How To Be

A

Successful

Camp Counselor

by **Dr. J. David Burrow**

McElroy Publishing
27-33 Fredonian St. • P.O. Box 488
Shirley, MA 01464

508-425-4055
800-225-0682

Copyright © 1998

by Dr. J. David Burrow

First Edition	January 1987
Second Edition	March 1989
Third Edition	March 1990
Fourth Edition	January 1992
Fifth Edition	February 1998
Sixth Edition	March 2000

ISBN 0-9622191-3-4

Table of Contents

Dedication

This book is affectionately dedicated to my dear mother, Mrs. Harriet Rigor, who sacrificially sent me to camp where dedication to Jesus Christ was learned. My mother moved into camping when her boys were in high school. She, too, became so "hooked" on camping that she went back every year as a counselor as long as I was in high school.

May the readers and their children enjoy the rich experience of knowing God's presence in a Christian camp.

Acknowledgments

I am grateful to my wife, Carol, who patiently read and reread the manuscripts. But far more imporant has been her faithfulness and support as I slowly learned the many lessons and principles that are now shared with you, my young co-workers in camping.

Without the dedicated effort of Jack McElroy, this book would not have come into existence. He is not only the publisher, he is a faithful friend who is not fearful of criticizing to make a good book better.

I wish to extend special thanks to Lynda Slattery for her fine, original illustrations. Her love for the Lord and for children comes through in her pictures.

Note: The use of "he", "his", "him", in some chapters is used as a grammatical neuter and is not intended to apply only to the male half of camp. Modern readers will have to forgive my old fashioned English. Wouldn't you agree that reading "he/she," "him/her," and "himself/herself" takes the fun out of reading an otherwise enjoyable subject?

How to Use this Book

Dear Counselor,

This is probably the most unique Camp Counselor Manual available today.   Why?

Because it is the only book that's been set up to be a pocket guide to give you quick and easy answers to a whole bunch of problems you'll probably run into here at camp.

The answers given and the methods outlined WORK. They've been developed over 20+ years of ministry.

If you follow the easy instructions given in this book, you'll enjoy the wonderful experience of being a Successful Camp Counselor!

Here's all you have to do...

Study the table of contents, and when you're faced with one of the problems listed there, turn to the section, read it and do what it says.

It's that simple!   When you've got free time, read over new sections and reread other sections.

You can read the book right through or jump around. It doesn't matter.   Just follow the instructions and may the Lord bless you as you serve Him!

Jack McElroy, President

Mc`Elroy Publishing

How to

1

Cooperate with God

It's easy to cooperate with God!

But before I tell you how, you need to know <u>why</u> it's so important.

1. What you do while here at camp may make the difference between heaven and hell for some of your campers.

2. If you cooperate with God, you are going to experience the most FANTASTIC summer of your life! You are going to experience God's working through you!

   You will know what it means to be used of the Holy Spirit to the glory of God.

3. You will experience the presence of God. He will be so real at times that you want to reach out and touch Him.

4. By cooperating with God, you are making yourself available to a God who is always searching for someone to "stand in the gap," to be ready for a special assignment, to be chosen of God to do eternal work.

This all sounds a little idealistic only because so few people let go of self and let God have His way. Unfortunately, you will probably see other counselors or staff who are struggling against the camp rules, tired of their assignment, not doing their best, or complaining. Pray for these friends, but don't follow them. They are not cooperating with God; and they are losing out.

"O.K., so how can I cooperate with God?"

The real key is your own attitude, or outlook, or approach to the ministry of camp counseling. In other words, it starts in your head and in your heart. Here are some basic things to keep right up front in your thinking:

1. You Have A Purpose

The purposes of the camp are to win youth to Jesus Christ, to build them up in Jesus Christ, and to further the molding of young lives after the image of Jesus Christ. As a counselor, you are here to accomplish these goals by caring, sharing, loving, helping and serving. As a counselor, you are in the pivotal position to accomplish these goals. These high and lofty goals are far removed from the base motivation of spending a summer at camp just to have a blast!

These purposes are so important that NOTHING must get in the way. If you or I or something else gets in the way, OUT it must go! Practical jokes get in the way, so OUT of camp they must go. We don't need them. Selfishness gets in the way, so OUT! Personal problems can get in the way, so let's cast them OUT (leave them at Jesus' feet) and get on with the ministry.

You will have the time of your life as a counselor, but when something (or a certain someone!) begins to hamper your ministry to the camper, it is time to put it aside and get back to the real purpose of your being at camp.

2. You Have A Plan

We accomplish our purposes by following our plans. The goals of the camp ministry are accomplished through prayer, Bible studies, programs, schedules, rules, people one-on-one, and devotions. Follow the plan! Your camp program will be well planned long before summer.

The Director and staff have a purpose for everything. Hundreds of details have been thought through in advance, so go with the plan and forget the complaining.

3. You May Have A Problem

People are the solution to make this camp effective, but people can be the biggest problem, too. People who do not understand or who don't have all the information may gripe, gossip, grumble, and grouch. They get their motives twisted, so they sow discord, spread negative undercurrents, and do the devil's work in the name of the Lord! While some people specialize in creating problems, why don't YOU vow to the Lord to be part of the solution. Be loyal to the Director and your supervisor. See yourself and EVERYONE else on the camp staff as part of the team functioning together in unity to accomplish God's purposes in young lives. God has called you to be a counselor, but his calling of another to clean the bathrooms or wash the pots is NOT a lesser calling, just a different one. Encourage and help one another. Stand together. Claim God's grace to give and forgive. If YOU can help create the right spirit in your camp, the Bible calls you a "child of God." (Matthew 5:9)

4. You Have a Fantastic Potential!

Being a counselor means giving, giving, giving. But did you know that as you forget about yourself and give yourself totally to the ministry of your campers that God Himself has special things to give you? Let me explain this very exciting part of the camp ministry: God's working in your life!

As a counselor, you will work harder than you do during most of the school year. Your day may start as early as 6:00 a.m. and not end until 10:30 or 11:00 p.m. But no one will be pushing or prodding you to do it. You will be expected to be on time, to participate, to cooperate, to do your very best all the time, but no one will be dogging your steps to keep tabs on you.

As a counselor you will succeed; you will win and will achieve. In your class there are no rejects, no failures, no loners, no leftovers. If you want all this, God wants to give it to you. Are you ready?

When you walk into camp, it may mean a whole new beginning for you. It's like a fresh start. Are you shy? Ask the Lord to make you more outgoing, and then take the first step by telling yourself, "Forget that shy routine; go up and talk to her. Lord, help me find two questions to ask to get it started."

Do you see yourself as a failure? Ask the Lord for success your first week. NO ONE FAILS unless he doesn't try and doesn't follow this manual. ("Lord, help me to do it right, for you.")

Whatever your past (i.e., hang-ups, pride, wrong motives, wrong priorities, personal problems), hang it on a nail outside of camp. THIS SUMMER you can be what God wants you to be. Put yourself in His hands. Let Him begin to mold you into that friendly, successful, sensitive, diligent servant of the Lord that you really want to be. God is able! Just get out of the way!

"Blessed are they which hunger (as a starving man) and thirst (as on a desert without water) for righteousness (doing it right) for they shall be filled." (Matthew 5:6)

Encourage and help one another. Stand together. Claim God's grace to give and forgive. If YOU can help create the right spirit in your camp, the Bible calls you a "child of God." (Matthew 5:9)

2

How to

Succeed the First Day

When a camper arrives in camp, it is the FIRST DAY of camp for that camper, even if it is the fifth or seventh week of camp for the counselor.

Counselor, <u>be fresh</u>, excited, enthusiastic, optimistic and UP! on every "first day" of camp.

Each camp has its own routine, but here are several basic principles that you will want to follow in order to get off to a good start.

As soon as a camper drives into camp, someone should greet him cheerfully and welcome him to camp. Help the camper's family feel right at home by helping them know where to park, where to go first, and so forth.

After the registration line, someone needs to be available to help carry the luggage. With all these "someones" much help is needed on opening day. You want to be available.

Make sure you introduce yourself and help the campers learn your name. It is even more important for you to learn each of <u>their</u> names. Take the time; it's worth it.

You are needed in the cabin. As the camper comes to your "home away from home," greet him with a big smile, "Hello!", and introductions. Let him choose his bed from those that are left; help him make it up, put away suitcases, and introduce him to all the others in the cabin.

Now you have a problem. "What do we do?" You can't leave the cabin because more are still coming through registration. Each camp should have its solutions, but here are some possibilities if you need more help.

What to Do During Registration Time

1. Have a simple game to play in the cabin. This will be needed if it's raining. It can be a group game like "20 Questions" or "Guess what I'm thinking of." It can be paper and pen games like "Tic-Tac-Toe," "Dot-to-Dot," or "Hang Man." Be ready with these extra resources.

2. Send the new campers off two by two. Send the "old" camper with a new one. The objective is to have the "old timer" introduce the new one to all the buildings and places in camp. Of course, you are also praying that a new friendship will develop.

3. Have a craft project ready in the cabin. Each camper could make a name tag and then wear it for two days. Make and decorate Bible verses for the walls. Make a cabin logo. Create a cabin cheer, a name, a poem, a goal for the week. Fix up the outside area of the cabin by raking, lining the path with stones, etc.

4. If it's a teen camp, use #2 and forget the rest. (They will want to do little more than talk and find out who is here again this year.) However, help the solo or loner camper to get "in" as quickly as possible. Don't leave him alone.

5. Give them free-time options. "You are free to do what you like until the bell rings. There is Ping Pong in the ___, shuffleboard down by the ___, crafts in the ___, basketball, ..." Make sure there is plenty to do. A few may want to help carry luggage or help in some other way.

You have survived registration. Now get the whole group together, reintroduce everyone, and move into the program.

What to Do on the First Day

That first day is critical. Everything that is done sets a precedent for the week. You want to win them to yourself during those first crucial hours. On the very first day, you will want to begin to express a love for each of your campers. This love is not based upon feelings or favorite campers. To love each camper, work on getting into the good habit of looking right into their eyes with love and acceptance. Talk with tones of acceptance and interest. Find an excuse to give a brief shoulder hug.

Avoid favoring the good looking, the cute, the personable, and the confident. They probably have others that give them love or attention. It's the unattractive that need your expressions of love the most.

Be careful that you not draw back from or tend to ignore the campers that "turn you off." Perhaps they are proud, crude, boisterous, ugly, fat, or foul. These kids need love as a fish needs water.

From that very first day, even while talking to the camper or observing him, **start to pray**....

a) for the camper -- for God's Spirit to move in that young life.

b) for yourself -- that you would know how to love each camper, know how to meet those needs, know how to relate to each one, and that you would have a genuine and deep concern for each camper.

When the camper first comes into the cabin, during that first meeting, what will he "read" from you as he/she observes your responses, your facial expression, your attitude, and how you relate to him/her.

The camper may see counselor reactions like these:

• "Camp would be more fun without you here."

• "I like you. Would you be my friend?"

• "Only one more week and I'll be out of this place!"

• "We are going to have a ball TOGETHER this week!"

• "Can I help you? I really DO care."

The basic question in the camper's mind is, "Does the counselor like me? Am I accepted?" If it's a teenage camp, they are asking these important questions about the peer group, too. Do everything you can to avoid a "reject" message being received by a camper.

The very first hour you will want to communicate the idea to every camper that he is important, accepted, secure, and headed for a wonderful week.

You do this by learning each name quickly, using the child's correct name (not nickname), listening (and learning!) when they talk, and showing genuine care for each one.

It is not the campers' responsibility to like the counselor. Some campers have a problem with anyone in the role of authority. Others (especially older teens) are very slow to warm up and trust you. It is quite dangerous to have the counselor dependent upon the camper's acceptance of him. What problems could develop in a cabin where the counselor had to have the camper's approval?

The initiative for love and acceptance is not on the camper, but on the counselor. Love, or acceptance, is never earned. The counselor (like Jesus Christ) just gives it.

Your first objectives on that first day are:

a) win that camper to yourself.

b) make the camper feel secure -- reduce fear.
(fear of new camp, new counselor, new kids, new program, new staff, new setting, new expectations, new rules, new peers, new leadership and authorities.)

In those first hours of camp, start immediately to learn all you can about each of your campers. How?

a) In conversation learn the name, background, and personality type (use key questions). Oldest in family? Youngest? First time in camp?

b) Observe how your camper interacts with others, talks or is quiet, confident or scared, outgoing or retiring.

c) Be alert to ways that you can move in to meet needs -- new friends, alleviate fears, make welcome, etc.

The first meal is important, too. What you allow or expect should be made politely clear. Help them with the camp's dining hall routine for entering, serving, cleanup, and leaving.

Never assume they know. Even the repeat campers may have done it wrong last year, or the procedures may have changed.

Never correct a child noisily for doing it wrong. Just show or remind him of the right way. Be positive.

Follow the same procedure for all the camp rules that first day or two. Do not yell or nag, just remind them of the right way and do not allow the wrong way.

In all things, remember that you love each child and that they came to camp to have a good time — help them.

WHAT TO DO WHEN YOUR CABIN GROUP HAS A W I D E CULTURAL VARIATION

By the time the last camper checks into your cabin you know that this camp session will be particularly difficult because you have a very wide range of cultural backgrounds: inner city, country, suburban, Asian, Middle Eastern, African, or a special religious group.

1. For younger children, there is so much in common in age group characteristics, that it may not make much difference. You only need to help them learn to accept each other's differences by appreciating the special God-given positive characteristics. Then help them have a good time doing something together.

2. If you are working with foreign students, encourage a spirit of, "We want to learn all about your country, and we want to enjoy teaching you about ours." This spirit is largely dependent upon the counselor's own attitudes.

3. If you have a mix of "street smart" kids and more culturally refined kids, you have a special problem. It will not be easy, but consider these possibilities:

a. Help them accept each other as being different but not one better than the other. <u>Kids do not have a choice on where they grow up</u>. The "straight" kids need some private counsel to encourage them to not look down on the inner city kids. <u>No</u> child needs more contempt or rejection!

b. Do not try to mix them. Let each go their own way. Why? Because the very nature of children is to always seek the lowest level. Parents will NOT appreciate their children coming home with the negative ways or language from other campers.

c. Whatever the cultural background may be, do not permit that which you know is wrong. This applies to language, actions and attitudes. You will need to establish clear guidelines the very first night. If you don't expect the best, you will never get it.

d. Lean heavily on the Christian kids to pray fervently for the others. Praying FOR them will work wonders in many ways:

i.. They will be more patient.

ii. They will tend to not copy the poor example.

iii. The Holy Spirit will honor honest and sincere prayer by bringing conviction to the heart.

iv. The ones being prayed over will not tend to be against the ones praying. You will have much better unity.

4. The Word of God is more powerful than your own arguments. If you have a strong cultural, ethnic, or behavioral variation in your cabin, emphasize the Scriptural standards by starting with an understanding of the very nature and character of God as being Holy.

Take every opportunity to teach the Word of God; and pray earnestly when your campers are under the teaching of the Word of God.

5. Use the Camp Director and Camp Pastor to counsel the camper leaders in your cabin who are causing the major problems. Get counsel from your camp leadership on how to deal with special campers.

What to Do on the First Night

The first night can be a problem, but need not be. The night routine that never fails will be discussed fully in another chapter. Let's talk about the particular needs of the first night.

Children's Camp

Sometime during the first day or at night just before cabin devotions, go over the rules. (See the chapter 7 on making expectations clear.) The rules you will cover as a cabin will be something like this if you have a gradeschool age group:

- "We are going to have a great time this week, and we are going to do it together."

- "We don't have a lot of rules, but one very important one is that we must obey. I must obey the Camp Director, and you must obey me. All of us must obey God. Why do you think this is so important?" Let them bring out the reasons for obedience. Weave in your objectives and the Scriptures.

- "Sometimes another cabin may be doing the wrong thing or be making a lot of noise when they should not, but WE will do what is right." Then talk over why God expects us to follow Him and do right, no matter what anyone else does.

- "We are going to be playing some great new games this week. In any game, someone wins and someone loses. What should we do if we win?" Talk about what it means to be a good sport in winning and in losing.

- It's appropriate at this point to give your cabin group a pep talk about being the best cabin. Frame "best" in Christian terms of conduct, honesty, alertness, obedience, cooperation, and so forth. Praise the idea of competition being far above points scored at a game. Measure being the best in terms of Christian character.

Teen Camp

In most teen camps, the weekly schedule gives the camper much more freedom. This means that your first night pep talk will take a different approach from the above points.

You may want to emphasize cooperation with you as a counselor and the other program leaders, standing for what is right no matter what others in camp do, or Christian sportsmanship when winning or losing.

Challenge them to be the BEST cabin in these areas as well as other camp competition.

The night routine (chapter 5) will work with this age group, too. However, you will need to know what is expected in your camp. In many teen camps, "lights out and quiet" may not be until quite late. Know your camp tradition. Know what the director honestly expects. It may not be the same as the schedule states. Keep your expectations of the campers on the same level as the rest of the camp. To be the only "hard liner" that sticks rigidly to the schedule could put you in a bad light with your cabin group on the first night.

Here they come, ready or not! Make that first day a GOOD day for every one of your campers. They are counting on you!

3   How to Handle Homesickness

There is a word that is never mentioned during camp, at least within earshot of any camper. The very mention of it causes a problem.

Many think this problem is more of a problem than it really is. If you plan and are ready for it, it need not be a problem at all. Since the word cannot be used, let's call it "it."

For you who are new on the camp scene, the "it" is sometimes spoken right out loud by parents. That's right! In the very presence of the child himself, the parent will even dare to suggest the possibility that their dear little child might be — homesick.

What causes "it"? A child's (or teen's) family is his emotional support. This emotional support is taken for granted until the child finds himself removed from it.

For many, camp is his first experience of separation. When at camp, the child may suddenly sense being stranded, alone. The ones he is used to having available are not there. PANIC! "I want to go home! I want my mamma!"

The feeling itself is quite real. "It" usually hits in the pit of the stomach and takes over the whole being.

However, "it" is primarily a mental or emotional problem and not physical. The real solution lies in solving the real problem.

The problem is a breaking away from traditional emotional support. The solution has two parts: establishing a new emotional support and growth toward independence.

The new emotional support system starts when the child comes into camp. Make him feel welcome and never allow him to be lost in the shuffle. Know his name, accept him, show him that you really care by listening to him, looking into his eyes, asking questions, and giving a caring hug around the shoulders. The camper must get the message that he is not alone. Security and love surround him.

Suppose chapel has just ended. It is getting dark. The whole camp family is walking toward their various sleeping quarters. "It" suddenly strikes Karen as she begins to think of her usual night routine at home. Darkness, cabin, trees, sounds, no dog, no mamma— PANIC! PAIN! TEARS! Then you come along side with a firm arm around the shoulder.

"Karen, wasn't that a neat story Uncle Jerry told us in chapel tonight?"

Her mind is in neutral or stalled out on self, so you continue, "We aren't finished yet. Lots of girls like the special time we have in the cabin after chapel."

Then you go on to dispel her fears by telling her exactly what will happen next. Reassure her of your presence all the time, tell about the funny thing that happened last week, or talk about that special day coming up tomorrow.

Above all, keep her moving and thinking about camp.

For most children that's all it will take. The sobs might last until sleep comes. You might step over to her bed after the "Last Amen" (see chapter 5) and pray with her a prayer of thanksgiving.

Thank the Lord for Karen, camp, good food, Uncle Jerry, the Bible teacher, new friends, ... and all the other good things at CAMP, not those at home.

Never mention or talk about home at all.

The next day, at lunch (because Karen is tired and her resistance is down) "it" starts all over again. Normally, just repeat what you did yesterday. Stall for one more day. "Let's get through today and then see how we feel."

But lets take it a step further.

Let's assume Karen is something of a problem. She starts to make a scene—will not eat, sobs continually, and insists on calling home and getting picked up today.

What to Do with a Camper

Who Insists on Calling Home

For the camper who has his mind set on calling home and/or going home, there is one basic approach that rarely fails.

You have already been kind and loving, so now you turn into a mild disciplinarian. With firmness that cannot be doubted, you look straight into those bloodshot, teary eyes and overlook the curled lip, and say: "Karen, your folks did not pay \$___ to send you here for one day. They expect you to stay the whole week. (This is a NEW idea for most campers!)

For your benefit, you CANNOT call home and you are not going home. So dry up those tears and get back with your cabin mates. You are staying. Is that clear? Then let's get going. This mild "get tough" approach works MUCH more effectively than piles of sympathy. In fact, using the motherly approach will often aggravate the problem.

Cutting off all hope of going back to the home support forces the child to strengthen himself and stand on his feet in a new context.

Exception: In consultation with your supervisor or camp director, it might be wise to call home to reassure the camper that "Mom wants me to stay." The camper may also need reassurance of parental love and protection (i.e., child abuse background, broken home, poor parenting skills). Follow this procedure: You, the camp nurse, or the camp director make the call. Explain the problem to the parent. Ask the parent to reassure the child that he/she is still loved, but the child must stay at camp for the week. Coach the parent to ask the child about the fun things that have happened already (put the camper's mind on camp). THEN ask the camper to come into the room and hand the phone to the child. Stay there and listen. When the child is done, take the phone back and confirm the parent's desires: "So it is all set that Junior will be staying the week?" Thank the parent and assure the parent of the good care the child is getting. Reassure the camper of the good times to come and that he/she is loved.

Another major help is to guide the camper into helping other campers. This takes the focus off himself. There may be a project or some need that he can meet. Try something like this:

"I've noticed that Jim is new at ping pong. You seem rather good. Would you play with him and help him practice?"

Occasionally, another option is to have the camper help a staff person with some work around camp. Do not overdue this approach or take the camper away from the program for a long time.

If you wrongly handle the child with this problem, and he goes home, the damage done will last for years. Usually, such a child will not survive a week of camp again.

If we were to take this problem one step farther, we would have a totally different problem. Very few children take the "it" problem to an extreme.

Those who do go to an extreme will not eat right, will not listen in chapel, will insist on their own way, will not try to get over it, and will <u>demand</u> they be allowed to phone home.

If you find yourself with such an obstinate child as this, send him to the Director. He is a discipline problem and needs to be handled as such. But do <u>not</u> turn against the child. Remember that you, the counselor, are always <u>for</u> the child and want what is best for him.

Two things bring on the problem of homesickness.

The first we have already discussed—an honest problem in establishing a new emotional support framework.

The second is the parent. With a few exceptions the really chronically ill children are preprogrammed by the parents. Parents will bid the child ado with parting promises, such as "I'm as close as the phone. Just call me if you get ___."

Then there was the parent who wrote about how everyone at home missed him, "And even the cat misses you." If the parent wants to destroy a child this way, there isn't much you can do. But try anyway, for the child's sake.

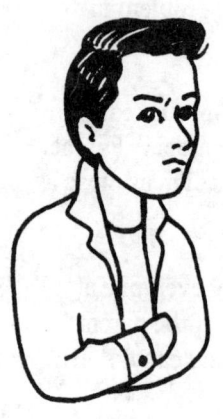

4 How to Make Goals for Campers

During this next week or two at camp, how will the camper GROW SPIRITUALLY? How will he GROW in CHARACTER? That answer is largely up to you.

Applying this chapter will make the difference between an average summer and a really great one. If the whole counseling staff will follow these guidelines, the camp itself will rise above the ordinary to the exceptional for three reasons:

1. Goals for campers will keep you focused on the real ministry and purpose of camp. It's easy to get sidetracked into program and fun or even problems. Goals help you keep going in God's direction.

2. Goals for campers help you see what is really happening right under your ministry. It's easy to miss! Goals will turn the spot light on God's working in your own cabin group.

3. Goals will keep you praying. The real work in a camper's life must be done by the Holy Spirit. Your earnest prayer brings that power into your campers' lives.

Your first goal is to understand the camper's needs. You can learn a lot by listening with both ears and casually, but intently, observing.

Listen. What is his vocabulary (i.e., street language, Sunday School, educated, slang, polite, crude, etc.)? How does he relate to others in the cabin (i.e., loner, leader, mischief- maker, follower, bully, wallflower)? How does he respond to you, the one who represents authority (i.e. clings, avoids, disobeys, obeys, ignores, pleases, deceives)? Look closely at his eyes, the window to the soul. What do you see (i.e. hurt, loneliness, fear, joy, confidence, life, peace, pride)?

If you can meet his parents, what do you see (i.e., wealth, poverty, character, cigarettes, Christian, confidence, fear ...)?

All of these observations are giving you clues to the spiritual needs in this camper's life.

Before the second day of camp (the first day is ideal) is ended, you need to <u>write down a goal</u> for every one of your campers. What do you want God to do in this individual's life this week? While closely observing each camper, ask God to give you divine insight to know what He wants to do this week in that child's life.

The Most Important Goal

Our first goal is that each child accept Jesus Christ as Savior. Each week at camp the camper will hear chapel messages on salvation, songs that deal with salvation, and Bible verses that point to salvation. But why does a child (or teen) respond or not respond?

The cycle goes something like this. We pray, and God hears that prayer. The Holy Spirit convicts of sin while the child is under the camp ministry of preaching, testimonies, and Bible studies. The child responds. God saves!

So who does all the work in salvation? (Hint: it isn't the counselor.) What is YOUR part? You, the counselor, are the example. You can also be the guide that shows the camper that Jesus

Christ is the answer. You may even be the one God uses to usher that camper into God's family!

You are the salt that creates a thirst for Jesus Christ. At the same time you are praying without ceasing for each child and giving the gospel message with an invitation during devotions or quiet time or even while taking a walk.

You are God's human instrument to accomplish His will.

Other Clear-cut Goals

The first goal is salvation for each child, but that's not the end. In fact, it's only the beginning. The next step is to discern how God would have that child grow in Jesus Christ THIS WEEK at camp. You create this goal for each camper from your observations and careful listening coupled with a sensitivity to God's direction.

Other goals could look something like this:

- That he would overcome shyness and get involved.

- That he would be considerate of other campers.

- That he would learn to be more gentle.

- That he would understand God's forgiveness of his sin so that he could learn to forgive others.

- That he would learn to pray.

- That he would not be rebellious.

- That he would be content (not complain).

- That he would start to read his Bible.

- The he would be more thoughtful of others.

- That he would be more compassionate.

• Any of the fruits of the Spirit.

• Any of the character qualities of Jesus Christ.

The list can go on and on with character qualities or changes in behavior that you see are needed. The important thing to do is to choose one main objective that you want God to accomplish in that child's life this week.

In choosing an objective, be realistic. Although God can do anything, He very rarely chooses to make a total transformation of a camper within one week.

What we CAN expect during the one short week at camp is some change, some movement in the direction toward which we have prayed.

Expect God to work and mold and change, but remember, the problems you see have been growing for eight to eighteen years. It will take time to undo the mess. Even Paul did not jump right into missionary work.

After you select a definite goal, <u>write it down</u>. This is essential. Writing it down will force you to make your objective clear, short, and reasonable. At the end of the week (or camping period), write down under the goal the RESULTS. What DID God do in the child's life this week?

The next step is to pray. Every day, at least three times a day, pray specifically for every camper by name. Pray specifically for the goal that you have set. No one else will have the fervency of prayer for your camper that you will have.

If there are others in the camp that you can trust to pray and not gossip, ask them to pray for your camper goals, too.

If you happen to have THE problem camper of the whole camp, get EVERYBODY praying for your camper: director, nurse, cook, dishwasher, life guard, lawn men, everyone. Then expect God to do something.

Oh, I should warn you about something at this point. If you have much fervent prayer going up to heaven for a "problem" camper, his behavior will probably get worse. Don't panic or doubt. Behavior usually does get worse where the Holy Spirit is convicting.

Just keep on praying, and be looking for opportunities to counsel. Every problem is an opportunity to counsel.

It really gets exciting to see how God has worked right in your cabin of campers! Write down the results. Give God an opportunity to prove Himself and to bless your heart! And rejoice when God did something special that you did not expect!

Ask the director if the whole staff could get together and rejoice over what God has done. If you're not setting goals and evaluating results, much of God's work in young lives will go unnoticed.

Goals Do Work

Some camps have a prayer partner system. The counselor is teamed up with someone else on the operational staff, and they pray together for the campers. Other camps meet as a total staff and pray together for campers.

When you find a need, set a goal, PRAY, PRAY, PRAY.

Summary

1. Goals for each camper are very important.

2. Listen, observe, and ask for God's wisdom to see the need (the goal that should be established).

3. Write down a clear-cut goal for each camper.

4. Expect God to work in every life.

5. Pray 3 times a day for each camper's goal.

6. Expect problems; use them to counsel campers.

7. Write down and share what God does in each life.

Any LASTING change in a camper's life will be a change that has been made by the Holy Spirit. You can measure your success as a counselor by the results of the Holy Spirit's work in your campers' lives.

5 How to Put a Camper to Bed

At Camp WaHoo the kids have a blast! The first night is spent in riotous living. "Lights out" occurs three or four times the first night, and finally the counselor goes to sleep so the campers don't have to listen to his, "Now this is the last time I'm going to tell you ...." About 3:00 a.m. the last camper sleeps from exhaustion.

The last night of camp has more order to it. The boys have planned a special party—without the counselor, of course, but including the girls.

The counselor rejoices at the grand cooperation and falls to sleep quickly. Then the fun really begins. When the staff members are coming back from THEIR party, they wake up the counselor and tell him that his kids are down at the lake with the girls. And God in heaven groans with disappointment that again the calling and pleading that He has done in young hearts has been thwarted by His own children, the ones He commissioned to bring the children unto Him.

If you want God to work in young lives, if you want teens to turn their lives over to God in a life-changing service or cabin devotional, then that young person needs to be mentally awake and emotionally stable. Getting a full night's sleep is essential to the accomplishing of these goals.

"Kids love darkness rather than light because the counselor can't see."

There is plenty of fun during the day, and perhaps a few well-orchestrated evening or night activities. Putting the camper to bed ON TIME and giving him (requiring?) a full night's sleep will not detract at all from the program of the camp and from God's program of conviction and growth.

You can do it without yelling and threatening. Actually, it can be fun! Anyone can do it. The following method has been successfully used for years with young people from the ages of 7 to 18.

Step 1: To the Cabin

The evening service or campfire has just ended. You're heading back to the cabin, which means BED for the campers. The game begins. "What can we do to avoid ending today?" is their goal. Your counter move is simply to WALK WITH THEM. Sound easy? Sure is! Unless you have a "special" friend who is counselor in the other half of camp. Campers first! Walk with them. Here's why.

1.   This avoids the need to scold later because they got "lost" going to the cabin.

2.   This gives another special opportunity to get to know them and their reactions to the meeting.

3.   You easily keep them moving in the right direction by moving in that direction yourself.

4.   It is a constructive way to give that personal attention and show real interest in individuals. You are establishing better rapport.

The only side trip for campers at this point may be to the nurse. Older ones can be sent. Younger ones may need to be taken or sent with a more responsible camper. Note: Do this NOW or else you will have a major interruption during devotions or even later.

Step 2: How to Handle the <u>First</u> Big Stall

You all made it to the cabin. Congratulations! Now, remind them of the next step. "Everyone get your toothbrush. We want to get to the washhouse before everyone else gets there!" Make it a game or contest if you can.

Now comes the first BIG STALL. Remember, the objective for the camper is to avoid at all costs that inevitable "lights out" time. He feels it coming closer, so he may try several maneuvers.

• "Who took my toothbrush! I left it right here!" Or the towel isn't around (it's on the line where he left it).

• He may just stand there, talk, and goof around with his buddy.

• As they fly out the cabin door, one may detour to the cabin next door.

• When finally AT the washhouse, rather than really washing up, the little water fight starts or a "deep discussion" on how the other team cheated (our team lost).

These are children (even if teens), so this behavior is normal. To counteract it, just patiently remind each one, ONE AT A TIME, what he OUGHT to be doing; then (now get this technique) just stand there and watch him until he does it. Simple, effective, and kind.

Please note that the counselor is WITH the campers the whole time. There is an art to getting through the night routine yourself

AND getting your campers through it. If you are working with a junior counselor, plan how to alternate the responsibility so both of you can be ready for the next step.

Step 3: Back to the Cabin

Getting some cabin groups through the wash-up routine is like trying to hold onto eight slippery fish. Don't give up, just keep praying for patience and perseverance.

The FIRST thing to do when a camper gets back to the cabin is to ask, "Did you go to the toilet?" Phrase it how you like, but make sure it is clearly understood. The rule is, EVERYBODY GOES. No excuses.

Step 4: How to Handle the <u>Second</u> Big Stall

He may repeat any of the methods used under #1.

The camper will not give a straight answer to your question because he knows that "I have to go!" is an excuse that never fails during cabin devotions, or later. Listen carefully for a straight and truthful response.

"I don't have to go." "I went after supper." Answer with a big smile or humor, but make it stick., "Try again, EVERYBODY goes."

At this point each one should be changing into his/her P.J.'s but some may be slow to the extreme. The basic rule is that NO CLOTHES are worn to bed that have been worn all day. For those not changing, try this:

"O.K., Joe, let's start with the shoes. Now the socks. Now keep going until you are in bed."

You stand there a few seconds and just watch until he really starts. If this does not work, go to the next step. "You either do it yourself or I'll have to do it for you." This is said with a big smile, of course. But stick with it! The farthest I've ever had to go was the shoes.

We need to pause here and make a special note. Some children are just embarrassed to change in front of others. So clue them in on how to do it under the covers quickly and quietly, rather than force them or ridicule them.

I've often told little guys, "Do it quickly <u>now</u>, everyone is changing and no one will notice." "Get back to the cabin early tomorrow night and be done changing by the time most get here." In any case, work WITH the child, and he will appreciate it.

Step 5: Into Bed!

Most are changed into night clothes. The bathroom visits have ceased. But as you look around the cabin, no one is in bed.

Give them a time limit or a goal. "O.K., in just 60 seconds I want everyone IN BED and ready to go to sleep, but we'll have devotions first before lights out." Most will enjoy the contest.

With older ones, you may need a few gentle but firm reminders: "Sam, let's get going. Don't hold up the cabin."

Help individuals (especially those that are slightly scatter-brained or disorganized) to quickly take care of last minute details and hop into bed. Work WITH them to meet the deadline and keep the countdown coming.

Once you get a camper into bed, don't let him get out!

Step 6: Devotions

We are speaking here of how to get campers into bed and asleep on time, so the discussion of how to conduct an evening cabin devotional time will be taken up later.

Start devotions even with a little noise in the cabin. Start with a memory verse review, a question, or something else. Do NOT start with prayer to get them quiet.

Prayer is a serious talking to God, not a technique for bringing order out of chaos. By the time you are done with this opening, you can "open" with prayer.

Step 7: The "Last Amen"

At the end of cabin devotions, encourage most of the campers to pray. Be sensitive to your group. "Old Timers" will usually pick up quickly and volunteer. Protect the "new kids" from being put on a spot.

Ask for volunteers, and then give an order of prayer. Finally give this little speech:

"Jim pray first, then Sam, Oscar, Red, Clem, any others? O.K., then I'll pray last. After I say "Amen", that's it for the night—no more talking or questions or bathroom visits." "Jim, would you start please."

So everyone closes his eyes, and Jim starts to pray. You may need to remind someone if he forgets he is next. At last you pray (KEEP IT SHORT, preach some other time).

Just before you do, or while one of the others is praying, you hit the light switch! Remember, they are all in their beds and ready to go to sleep (you hope!). So you say, "Amen."

"O.K. guys, this is our last ditch effort to stall off going to bed!" is the thought in several young, creative minds. Counselor, are you ready for—

Step 8: How to Handle the Third Big Stall

1. "I have to go to the bathroom!" "Me too!" Did he go before? Did you, as counselor, make SURE he went? Then you have one pat answer: "No." Of course, if you forgot to ask him, he has you. You lose, and he wins.

If that is the case, send them ONE at a time. If you DID check one at a time and he said he DID go, then you tell him, "No, you will have to wait till morning." He says, "But I gotta go" and breaks the whole cabin up with laughter.

At this point I pull out my old standard reply that has become a standing joke in my camps: "Sorry, no deal. Medical records prove that you can wait 12 hours without any physical harm. If there is a mess in the morning YOU can clean it up."

In short, hold your ground!

2. Following this go-round or instead of it, there are all kinds of "important" comments or wise cracks to cabin mates . Some even try the old "Good night Sam, Good night Ollie, ..." and go around the cabin. Then the next one picks it up and does the same.

3. Of course, now the campers get very respectful and want to ask you, the father or mother of all wisdom, some important questions.

Girls often appear to get very spiritual at this point.

For all these important questions and comments, you have only one stock answer: "I said that's it for today, no more talking tonight." "I'll answer that tomorrow, not tonight. Good night." or "Sh-sh-sh, no more tonight, tomorrow's another day."

---

4 Rules the Counselor Must Keep to Make It All Work.

Remember, once you answer a question, you have broken your own rule about talking, so, MANY other questions will follow. YOU said "no more talking"; therefore, the most important rule is this: *YOU cannot continue a conversation either.*

Beware of this trap. MOST COUNSELORS fall for this one and the kids know it.

The second basic rule is not obvious: *Always speak quietly to the individual who is talking, NOT to the group.*

Say as little as possible yourself, say it softly, and say it only to ONE person. Never again, the rest of the night, will you address the cabin as a whole. ALWAYS speak only to the one person.

"Why?" The mental game they play is this: "He is really speaking to the others, so I am getting away with it." You crash their game when you address them by name: "Harold, no more. We are done."

If you have five talking, go to each one's bed and give him the same message with just a little variation. "No matter what the others do, YOU quit. No more."

The <u>third rule</u> is this: you must *stay on your feet* in the middle of the cabin. If you were sitting on your bed when you said "Amen," stand up in the middle of the dark cabin immediately. Just stand there.

For each disturbance, go to that person's bunk and speak to him. Being on your feet will help you get quickly and quietly to where the problem is. An added benefit is that the whole cabin will be quiet to hear what you are telling Harold in his ear!

The <u>fourth rule</u> must also be kept: *Stay in the cabin*; do not leave. If you leave now for that staff party (or special "friend"), the alert camper will assume leadership and start his own party.

In any case, every camper must ALWAYS have some responsible adult there. It is a basic of good child care. Never leave campers alone. NEVER.

"Our Last Chance"

So you won the first round, but these campers do not intend to give up! "O.K., so he's got us on the talking routine, but let's try another angle."

Step 9: How to Handle the <u>Fourth</u> Big Stall

(THE BIG JOKE)

Usually it comes after devotions and often after the talking has stopped. The little geniuses will start with the mouth noises, rubbing or bumping the wall, crinkling paper, throwing little objects to a friend, playing with a flashlight, or the methodical rolling back and forth in the squeaky old army bed.

Hang in there, counselor, you WILL win the game!

1. Stay on your feet in the middle of the cabin. When you know who is doing it, go to that ONE person and tell him to stop (the action) because it's time to go to sleep, not play games. Part of the game he is playing is, "Does the counselor know what I'm doing." You won the game!

2. If you need to calm a camper down, speak ever so softly close to him and give him a lecture that would put anyone to sleep! Tell him he's been a good camper; it's been a good day; let's end the day right; much to do tomorrow so we need a full night's sleep; it is not right to keep the others awake, etc.

When Can You Go to Bed?

IF you will use this method, you will find that you will be getting much more sleep. In fact, all you want.

You are on your feet in the middle of a dark cabin. Several campers have had the pleasure of your personal visit. The games seem to have ended. You won! Your next step is to listen.

Listen for that slow rhythmic breathing. You'll hear your campers "pass out" one at a time. At last only two or perhaps three campers still have that mild restlessness. Safe? Almost.

Sit down on your bunk. If you have Old Squeaky, the campers will hear it. But they are listening for TWO squeaks, not one.

It takes one to sit and TWO to lie down. Just sit for another five minutes, then lie down with your eyes on that one camper that you are not sure about. Another five minutes and you are safe, but do NOT leave the cabin! The squeak of the door is the "GO!" signal to start another party because the counselor is gone!

Some counselors have come back to a cabin with the lights on, everyone up, and the rather obvious remains of a pillow fight. If you DO leave the cabin, leave someone else standing in the middle of the floor.

If you have seven and eight-year olds, you may need to take a second trip to the bathroom about 30 to 60 minutes after the "Last Amen". When they finally slow down and relax, bedwetting can be a real problem. With eight campers, you may have one to three campers with this problem.

One morning a young boy asked me, "Uncle Dave, didn't you go to bed last night?" I was still standing in the middle of the cabin when he got up! Of course, I had a good eight hours sleep, too.

Obviously, after this routine has been established, you will be able to sack out much sooner. If you happen to have that rare ideal cabin, you can say "amen" and go to sleep yourself.

Some girls' cabins gather around on a couple of bunks for devotions. If the girls are giving a high level of cooperation, that's fine. What has been herein described is the course to take when all is not so rosy.

Remember Ecc. 5:12 "The sleep of a laboring man is sweet." Good night.

What to Do if Your Camper Wets the Bed—
How to handle this accident.

Bedwetting, or enuresis, can ruin a camping experience for a child (and the counselor!). If you have a camper with a history of bedwetting, be calm, and do not make the camper feel guilty. Handle the problem with a matter-of-fact attitude.

If a camper has had an "accident" during the night, he or she will be embarrassed. It is up to you to IMMEDIATELY take steps to alleviate the camper's anxiety. You should assist the bedwetter in as quiet and unobtrusive a manner as possible to wash or change the bedding and take a shower. Sanitize the mattress.

Care needs to be taken to prevent the bedwetter from becoming an object of ridicule in the cabin. Develop a signal so the bedwetter can comfortably ask you for help. Perhaps bedding can be changed or aired while your other campers are occupied elsewhere.

To prevent bedwetting:

1. On hot days, encourage plenty of drinking during the day. At supper limit liquid to 8 oz, and no drinks at the snack shop afterward. Children with this problem often drink heavily within two hours of bedtime; that's trouble!

2. Make sure this camper makes a good effort in the bathroom during the night routine.

3. Get the camper up 45 minutes to 1 hour after falling asleep and take him (or her) to the bathroom.

Bedwetting is very embarrassing. Most campers will be very grateful for anything you do to help them prevent the problem.

6

How to
Conduct Cabin Devotions

Probably the time that is most remembered in camp by both counselors and campers is that special time at the end of the day when the cabin finally quiets down and talks seriously about spiritual matters. At least, it COULD be the best time of the day.

Too often it degenerates into another preaching session with the counselor as the preacher and the campers, his captive audience.

If one needs to practice his preaching, however, I would suggest the corn fields.

Many first time or young counselors nearly panic at the thought of this time. "What do I say? What do I do?"

As often as I have stood in a cabin with boys snug in their beds and eyes asking "What are you going to do?", there are still times when some level of panic comes.

However, let's approach this as one of the most significant parts of the day that we want to use wisely. It's really not bad if you start to plan this time with this prayer: *"Lord, what do you want me to do and say? I yield myself to Thee. Use me."*

Before you even reach the cabin with eight sticks of dynamite (campers), there in your head, if not on paper, must be the basic content of your devotional time.

Some counselors plan it during rest hour. Others scratch notes during vespers. Some plan it as they walk from chapel to the cabin. A few may even bring a book of some type with ideas and outlines all ready. Whatever the case, be prepared.

Four Steps to Successful Devotions

Step 1:   **Establish a goal.**

What do you want to accomplish? Is there a response you want? A new understanding of something? A new seed thought to plant? A problem that needs to be worked out or discussed? If the time is late (the meeting ran far overtime), the goal may simply be to close out the day by talking with the Lord.

If you have ever helped your family when traveling, you used a road map. It was a mess of lines all over the paper, but you saw a starting point and an ending point. To reach your goal, you must keep going toward your destination. With each detour, you must plan how to get back onto the best road that goes the shortest way toward your goal.

So it is with cabin devotions. You need to keep your mind on the goal, and with each sidetrack that the campers take, quickly plan on how to reach your destination (goal) from the new place where you are.

To have devotions without a goal is to try to reach a destination IN A GIVEN TIME without a road map. You do not have all night to reach your goal!

Even with a longer devotional time, the attention span of your campers gives you a very definite time limit. Use your time wisely. Keep going toward your goal.

Step 2:   Start the devotional time.

When you start will depend on a combination of the clock and the state of readiness of the cabin. As noted earlier, when we detailed the going-to-bed routine, all the campers should be in bed.

If you have them in bed and the schedule says it is nearly time, get started. Many times I have started with one camper still getting ready by just ignoring him and getting the attention of the rest.

You could start by reviewing the verse of the day in unison. This gets everyone together and stops the chatter.

Another method is to use an open-ended question: "What did you like best about chapel tonight?" "What was the best part of the Bible story this morning?" "Which are your favorite songs?" "Who can give me one verse that tells us to be kind to others?"

After asking the question, you allow only one to answer at a time and remind the others to be courteous and listen.

Step 3:   Content.

There is something you want to get across, something you want to teach. Be careful for a clever trap here. Be sure that all your teaching is based on the Bible.

We all have our IDEAS and opinions, but that is not what the campers need. When a question comes up, base your answer on Scripture or Scriptural principle.

All of your campers should have their Bibles in bed with them at this point, so have them look up the verse or read it together. Let them see for themselves that the answers to life's problems are found in the Bible.

(The "Seven Basic Principles" that follow give more detail about how to plan the content section)

Step 4:   Close the devotional time and draw conclusions.

If you have had a discussion, wrap it all up in a summary. Make your goal clear at this point. Now is the time to give that invitation.

"All of you close your eyes for a moment. I want to ask a question that is just between us. Tonight, for the first time, would any of you like to ask Jesus Christ to come into your heart, take away your sin, and take over your life? Would you just raise your hand as you lie there in bed?"

If you do get a response, go into the "Last Amen" routine. If there are two counselors, one of you takes the child outside (if it's warm and dry) and goes over the plan of salvation.

If this is not good for your situation, finish the "last Amen" and then go over to that child's bunk in the dark and talk to him. If it is Holy Spirit conviction, it will also be there tomorrow morning.

Seven Basic Principles

Principle 1: Base all teaching on Scripture, not opinion.

Principle 2: Involve the campers.

Another preaching session they do NOT need. Even if you are a preacher, the effectiveness of this particular hour will be limited with the lecture approach.

Remember, they probably just came from Vespers where preaching was experienced for an hour. If you want them to look forward to devotions, involve them. Usually, that involvement means leading a discussion. How to lead a discussion is covered in the next chapter.

(For more ideas for camper involvement see #7 below and the following chapter, How to Have a Discussion)

Principle 3: Stay on the track.

Remember that high school teacher you had who could easily be taken off the track? My English teacher was good at juggling, so the earlier class clued us in that he had been juggling ink bottles. With some effort, we got him sidetracked again. Anything but English was our goal.

Some of your campers may have the same idea. Some kids are quite good at it, almost professional, in fact. They start talking about their friends or family back home, the ball game today, the cookout, the spider on the ceiling, and (this is always a great one for the girls' cabin) "I saw a MOUSE!"—scream, yell, jump, panic.

If the attack is not so direct, they may try the "spiritual" questions or curiosity questions from the Bible. If you can discern that the question is coming from a genuine concern or if the question is a very worthy topic to cover, you may want to totally scrap your planned devotional and quickly establish a new goal with new content.

For example, in the junior-age years, heaven is a genuine concern. If heaven suddenly is a bright spot of interest, change to that one.

The Bible should be familiar enough to you so that a proper reference could be found. If this topic is brought up on the first night of camp (or if you plan ahead and use it then), how fitting would be an invitation to salvation after going through the plan of salvation (how to get to heaven).

Most decisions for salvation come on the first or second night of camp.

Principle 4: Beware of the questions that really cannot be turned into a Scripture dig.

Many questions are not directly or clearly answered in the Bible (i.e., Where did the dinosaurs come from? Did they really find Noah's ark?) Reply: "Let's talk about that when we are waiting in line for lunch tomorrow." That particular question could also be turned into a study on creation.

Principle 5: Some things to avoid while giving devotions.

Avoid talking over the campers' heads. It is hard to gear a devotional for a particular age group. This involves a topic that is relevant to the age, words that are understood, and a level of knowledge that is already acquired.

Many times certain vocabulary words can be defined so the campers can stay with you. If you want to really communicate, they have to be able to understand. Avoid embarrassing a camper by asking him to read from the Bible. You better know his reading ability first, even in high school.

Review: Avoid preaching. Avoid sidetracks. Avoid empty curiosity questions. Avoid major distractions.

Principle 6: Close with the procedure of the "Last Amen."

To have a small riot after devotions is to destroy that which you hoped to accomplish. Many a night in camp has closed with a spiritual discussion, and a few minutes later that cabin is raiding another cabin.

Principle 7: Use variety.

What can you do in the devotional time besides preach? You can discuss as a group, give each a verse or two to look up, ask one question and then go around and have every person answer it, tell a story, use a visual, try an object lesson, use a devotional book (NOT every night, please), or have the campers give the devotional (plan ahead and use this with older children).

Giving a cabin devotional is nothing to panic about at all. Whatever you give to the children, give from your heart and life. Don't try to fake it and give what God has not given you.

Talk about prayer if praying to your Father is oh so real to you. Talk about God's care if you have experienced His providential hand taking care of you. Let the devotional flow from your heart, and it will touch their hearts. But keep it in the Word of God.

Five Nights of Sample Topics

Here are some EXAMPLES to try in cabin devotions. This will never do for a whole summer, but some of these may work for you and get you started. Change them to meet the needs of your groups and to meet your goals.

Monday Night

This is a general opening up discussion. Their answers cannot be wrong. Everyone will participate. If they don't, coach them into answering: "Jerry, I'd sure like to know what you think. Can you tell us?"

"Why did you come to camp? What do you hope to get out of this week?" Lead from these questions into suggestions for getting the MOST out of camp by seeking the Kingdom of God (God's rule and reign in each life). Point up the great spiritual opportunities. Center this devotional around Matthew 6:33.

Tuesday Night

"Everyone get your Bibles before getting into bed. Now, look up a Scripture verse or small section of Scripture that you really like. Find something that is meaningful to you." Give them a few minutes to find it. "Let's go around the cabin, read the Scripture loud and clear, and then tell us WHY it's a verse you like, or tell us what it means to you."

As they do this, help the whole cabin understand the meaning of each verse. Encourage each camper to tell more about his own personal faith in Jesus as he explains the PERSONAL significance of this verse to himself.

You are finding out about each camper and where he is spiritually, and you are letting campers preach to campers. Kids need to know that other kids really have something.

Wednesday Night

By this time of the week, it would be a good idea to use I Cor. 13 and apply it to the camper's relationship to everyone else in camp. Pick out of the chapter the need that your group has evidenced. The following question is only an example.

"Let's assume that we are Christians and that we are going to live the kind of life that is described in this chapter while we are at camp. When are some times that we should be patient with each other?"

Point out times when they are in line and have to take turns, or times when the life guard or teacher makes a mistake like blaming them for something they did not do. Above all, get out of the general and into the SPECIFIC.

Thursday Night

This is near the end of the week (already!). Does salvation need to be pressed home? Dedication? Forgiveness? Take a topic from the lives of campers as you have seen a need develop.

Friday Night

Assuming this is the last night, encourage them to talk about what they have learned spiritually this week. Were any decisions made? This is a time for testimonies, so let the campers speak (that means the counselor is quiet—not preaching).

Encourage them to pray for those in camp who are not saved or not living a life worthy of the Lord.

ENJOY this time! It's often the most important part of the day.

7

How to Have
Effective Discussions

What <u>Not</u> to Do

Have you ever played, "Guess what I'm thinking"? It's a game where the leader has the answer in mind and the others are trying to guess it.

If you try to have a "discussion" by asking a question with a specific answer, most people will not take the risk of being wrong; so no one will answer even the simplest question. A good discussion leader must avoid any semblance of this game!

Two Things That Should Happen in a Good Discussion.

• Have participation. The more they participate together; the more interest, attention, and results will come from the Bible study.

• Learn more about each child as they talk or respond. LISTEN with both ears and mind. Everything he says is telling you something about himself. By listening, you are beginning to understand where each child is spiritually, mentally, socially, and emotionally. This gives you direction in planning your next cabin devotional time or in planning your one-on-one talk.

Three Types of Camper
Response and What to Do with Each

The first is "The Talker." This person goes on and on and often just in circles. You will have to politely cut this person off, after giving him ample time to get his point across.

The second is the quiet one. He doesn't say anything, so ask him personally. "Herk, what do you think this man in the story was trying to do?" You might be amazed at how the quiet ones often come up with the greatest insights.

Third is the wrong answer child. He just can't seem to get on your track of thinking. Try to pick out the correct part of his response and repeat it with praise to the child who gave it. Or give him credit for being so close or for having a good idea.

In any case, NEVER be critical or call attention with any emphasis to any response that was wrong.

When a correct answer or response is given, give a clear word of praise or encouragement, then repeat in the exact words of the camper the key phrase or sentence so everyone can hear it.

> When you repeat the correct answer, USE THE EXACT WORDS the camper used. Do not change anything or substitute any synonyms. Doing this adds great worth to the response and will greatly encourage others to respond.

"Guess what I'm thinking of" puts worth only on the idea of the leader, rather than putting great worth on the ideas of those participating. The difference between these two approaches will make a vast difference in the amount of participation.

How to Get Kids Talking

If you want discussion, you need a question. The concern then becomes, "What kind of question?" We already buried "Guess what I'm thinking of", so let's move on to something that works.

Open-Ended Questions

Use an open-ended or opinion question like "Who do you think is the greatest man in the Old Testament and why?" Each child may have someone else in mind. Praise each one for picking such a great man and repeat something of what the child gave for a reason of why he was great.

DO NOT end up with, "Those all are good, but I think the greatest man is David. David..." In so doing, you just shot down their worth and proved you were looking for a particular answer. The next time, they may not be so quick to answer you.

Instead, use this summary: "You have really chosen some great men: David, Samuel, Moses, Joseph—can you think of anything that was true about ALL of these men?" Can you put yourself as a participant in this group and feel why you would be encouraged to participate? If you want to emphasize a particular point (as from the second question), you could say: "I like what you said about how each man is courageous. Can we be like that this week?"

Now you are guiding the discussion instead of killing it. You are not going back to preaching.

Research Questions

For some more seasoned campers (or other groups), you can use research questions. Have them look up a Scripture and then explain the results to the group. This can even be used with junior age if the question is down at their level.

For example, give a particular chapter to look up and ask open questions like, "How was this man kind to someone he did not know?" "If you were in his place, how would you have felt?"

Mystery Guest

This method can be used during rest hour, if you have 15 minutes together before a meal, or in evening devotions. This method is to review what has been taught in Bible class or the evening service.

Give one camper a slip of paper with a Bible person's name, a Bible principle, or a Bible event that they just learned. The rest of the cabin asks this camper "yes" or "no" questions, until one camper can guess who (or what) the mystery guest is. If the camper guesses wrong, he is out of the game until the next guest.

If you start your evening cabin devotions with this method, you could have just one "guest," and then use that as a spring board or foundation upon which to build your devotional time.

The Debate

Divide the cabin into two groups. Propose a question or problem and assign one group "against" and one group "for" (or two different positions on the question). The counselor is the moderator. The counselor should create a debate issue that will help the cabin group think through an issue.

Remember, any debate should come back to the Scriptures. After the campers' debate, the counselor may need to refocus their thinking back on the Scriptures that give some guidelines. OR, the counselor could give these select Scriptures to each side to be included in the debate.

A few examples:

"Should Dave have obeyed his brothers and gone home?"

"Should we forgive someone who continues to be mean to us?"

"Should we just hang around with our old friends?"

"We should be able to watch any TV that we want."

"Should everyone be a missionary?"

After the debate is over, the counselor should summarize the main points and generously praise those that participated.

"I Need Advice" or "What Should I Do?"

The counselor explains to the camper that he wants the campers to be his counselor (just for fun). He has a problem, and he needs their advice. After the counselor explains his problem, he tells his campers: "That's my problem. Now what should I do? One person at a time give me advice, and then that person call on the next counselor." When a camper finishes giving his advice, that camper chooses who will speak next.

For the problem, that counselor should create a make-believe story that would parallel a situation that might be real for this age group of campers. (For example, her best friend is not paying attention to her because another girl is now the best friend.) The counselor should really play the part and describe the problem as a camper would do it.

When the campers are giving advice, the counselor should respond with questions and objections. If the campers can handle it, don't be too easy on them.

This method will help the campers think through a problem as well as feel with the adults who are constantly trying to solve children's complaints that are often based on selfishness and rebellion.

The Panel of Experts

Select three or four of the sharpest campers and set them up as a panel. You could also choose four bunks that are close together.

Propose a question to the panel (similar to one of the questions or issues in the methods already enumerated). The rest of the cabin group then asks the panel how to solve the problem, or what Scriptures would apply, or "what if" questions.

The panel are the experts. The cabin group wants the answers.

Read and Question

Select a passage of Scripture that you want the cabin group to read aloud and together. Choose Scripture that will fit their level of reading ability, and choose less that 20 verses total.

As they read the Scripture aloud and together, stop them after every one or two verses and ask questions related to what they just read. If you are dealing with a problem that you have in your cabin group, this can focus the attention on the problem and the solution by letting them do the preaching. There are many more possible questions, but here are a few to get you started:

"Why did he do that?"

"What if we did that. What do you think would happen?"

"Have you seen an example of that today?"

"Is that what people usually do? Why not?"

What to Do When It Does Not Work

Sometimes you can do everything right and nothing happens. There just is not the cooperation or interest or response or attention for which you hoped. Before putting yourself in the stocks, take a more objective look at the total situation. There may be other causes. For example:

1. Are you wound up tight, disturbed, and thus not showing real love and concern for the campers?

Your mind could really be on your home problems, girl friend problems, or other personal problems. The campers may pick up the tone and read, "He really doesn't care."

The solution is to simply pray and get yourself straightened out with the Lord. "Lord, I commit that problem to you. Now empower me to minister as I should right now." Of course, if there is sin, you'll have to take care of that. (I John 1:9 and restitution, if needed).

2. You may be talking too much ("Perish the thought! How could THAT ever happen with ME?"). You just need to stop long enough for them to think (don't let the silence scare you). Come back to the question method and wait patiently.

3. The campers may be wound up, excited, and not at all ready to settle down. This is often true on the first night and at weekend retreats. You can calm them down by reading scripture (try Psalm 119) or by reading a story (even OLDER ones like it).

You could spend more time going over the Scripture for the day. On the first night, you will need time to go over the cabin rules and give your pep talk. If all else fails and the group just is not with you in your discussion and devotions, cut it short and have a longer prayer time.

Send for help, too. The person just above you on the organizational chart should be available to help. In any case, do NOT scold and chastise or criticize the children; the supervisory staff is available to help you.

4. The children may be just too tired and have no energy left to listen by the end of the week. Put them to bed earlier and have SHORT devotions before prayer time, especially with younger children. You may want to just have a prayer time, and skip the sermon. (This point is not applicable to teens).

5. There may be something in the cabin that is keeping them going: mouse, fly, wasp, moth, spider, branch scratching the roof, night sounds in the woods. If you can't really get rid of the distraction, assure campers of God's care and protection, then turn the lights out and continue. Get their minds off it.

Again, put your pride in your pocket and send for help if you need it.

6. You may have one or two campers who are definitely a problem. They have no discipline at home and are often trouble at camp. Now they are making devotions nearly impossible. Try solutions # 3, 4 or 5. Or, give a first warning and then a second, and the third time put them on the front steps of the cabin with a junior counselor.

I have had some campers "cool their heels" on the front step of the cabin for 45 minutes. Finally, they got bored with the quiet and decided to go to bed peaceably.

For most problems there is a solution. Work with your fellow staff members as a team to find just the right solution for your situation. Give your best to the campers by getting the help you need.

Summary

Time to have a discussion?

Plan carefully.

What is your objective?

What will be the Scriptural foundation?

What will be the physical setting?

Which methods described in this chapter would work best?

Any method that you have not used before will take some practice in developing it into a useful tool. Try each of the methods suggested on different occasions. Practice using them several times until you feel comfortable. Adapt them in ways that will work better with you and your situation.

If it doesn't work well, rethink the questions you used, the approach you took, and the other factors that have drilled holes in your ship. But do not give up!

8   How to Have Good Manners In Camp

Camp is a friendly, informative, fun, and often lighthearted place. Young folks come to have a good time, meet friends, and learn new things. When at the table in the dining hall, eating is a special time of fellowship and frolic.

But, we are not in just any camp; we are in a CHRISTIAN camp. Something is different here. Jesus Christ is Lord.

Yes, even in the dining hall, Jesus is Lord. Our Lord would always have his children use good manners because He taught us, "Be ye kind one toward another," and "Love one another as I have loved you." Being discourteous just does not fit that standard.

During a counselor training session before the camp season, I asked the counselors (who had been divided into small groups) to write down the answers to some specific questions on manners.

Keep in mind that at this camp we used only family style dining. The following is the list of answers given to each question.

"What manners and courtesies can we expect of campers at the table?"

- Pass the food to the person to your right instead of reaching.

- Food is for eating, not for throwing or playing.

- Quiet talking is used instead of yelling.
- Remain seated at the table until dismissed.
- Wait to eat until everyone is served at your table.
- Salt, pepper, and sugar containers are not toys.
- Use your fingers only for finger foods.
- Don't lean back in chairs.
- No elbows on the table.
- Put napkins in the lap and use them.

- Strictly observe the quiet rules. (When a small bell is rung, everyone is to become quiet.)

- Share. Take only your portion. (In family-style eating, a platter of food should go all the way around the table with everyone getting something before seconds are brought.)

- Everyone takes at least one "no-thank-you" portion. (In this camp, everyone had to eat at least a spoonful of what was served. Very often, after one spoonful, the camper wanted more.)

One might guess that the counselors who answered these questions had some experience. We can begin to see how having good manners is really just a way of being thoughtful and kind to others.

"What manners and courtesy should campers show toward each other?"
- Do not argue. Be agreeable.
- Help others with jobs to be done.
- Respect each other's property.
- Use each other's proper name.
- Be quiet while others are sleeping.
- Be kind to one another. Be sensitive to other's feelings.

This particular list also gives some ideas to cover in cabin devotional periods. Can you see some problems that these counselors have faced in their experience with campers?

"What manners should be commonly used between the counselors?"

- Be respectful. Do not criticize, talk down, or belittle the other.
- Use much mutual encouragement. Everyone needs it!
- Give each other space -- physically and emotionally.
- Do not bother to argue. It's better to give in or keep quiet.

- When appropriate, use teamwork. Use each other's strengths. Be quick to help each other when asked.

- Be kind and thoughtful. The other person could be having a hard day or have a much more difficult group of campers.

- No gossiping. You will learn many things about each other; and some things are better kept to oneself and not repeated.

"What manners should be shown between the counselor and the Director, Program Director, etc.?"

- Cooperate with them and encourage the campers to cooperate.
- Do not talk against them and joke against them.
- Give them respect.
- Keep campers under control. Quiet them down.
- Give them full attention.
- Ask them if there is anything that can be done for them.
- Help with the games or other activities.

"What manners should the girls on staff show toward the other girls on staff?"

- Be polite.
- Don't criticize their way of doing things.
- Don't gossip to or about them.
- Respect their feelings and beliefs.

- Be quiet when others are sleeping. Some need to get that early afternoon rest

- Respect other's property. It is right to NOT borrow another's things or take advantage of them.

Manners -- How Much Can be Expected?

Be realistic and don't go to extremes. That in itself is manners. If it is kind, it is good manners. How far should you go with manners?

That will depend on your cabin group. That sweet little group of girls that just drips with honeyed sweetness will love your counsel on how to develop more refined manners.

But those eleven-year old boys who are all body and no coordination will be doing well to keep the milk upright on the table, and to manifest enough self-control to keep from pushing Peggy Pigtails out of line.

Camp is fun. If you can make manners fun, go as far as you can! If you have a difficult, or rather uncultured group, demand the minimum. You are the counselor.

And the manners that <u>you</u> need to exercise toward others? You will always feel good about doing what is right. It's truly a pleasure to have good manners towards others, no matter what they may do.

9 How to Understand Camper Behavior

Four Basic Factors

There are four basic factors that generate behavior patterns. Each one is significant, but each child is a special and unique mix of all four. In any one child, you may find one factor that dominates all the others.

The **four factors** are:

- Behavior that is characteristic of a given age group.

- Behavior that is learned from the cultural and family context.

- Behavior patterns growing out of the birth-order sequence in the family unit.

- Behavior patterns that are characteristic of a personality type.

How Age-Group Characteristics Affect Your Campers

Some books or booklets have age-group characteristic lists. These were lists of things common for each general age of children.

These charts can be quite helpful, but as a counselor, I had problems remembering the lists! If you have such a chart and it helps you, great! With or without such a list, the following project will become more meaningful than pre-made charts.

How to Profile Each of Your Campers

At the beginning of each rest hour when the campers are quieting down, or during some other quiet time during the day when you can observe your campers, take out a clipboard and piece of paper. Make a list of the common behavior patterns that you have noticed in your group of campers.

If you have a wide age span in the same cabin group, make a separate list for each age. You will begin to notice things that are common to most of the children of any given age.

For example, your list may include things like this: giggles a lot, stays in groups of three, is rarely alone, looks to the others for approval, works hard, is cooperative, is eager to please, is very noisy, is continually active. You may be amazed at how much they all act alike!

If you will do this project and add to it each week, your real understanding of children will take a huge jump. As you understand them more, you will have more patience.

You will also have the ability to spot the exception, the troubled child, the immature, the advanced, the leader, and the late bloomer.

On your day off or between camp sessions, compare notes with other counselors who have the same aged campers. It will be fun and a giant learning experience.

If you are a college student, this project will be good for a super term paper in the Childhood Development course.

How Culture and Family Affect Your Campers

Cultural and family background will have a major impact on a child's behavior. If a child grows up in the big city, his interests, language, values and experiences may be quite different from the well-off suburban child. How do you think a divorce in the family would impact a child? Is your camper from an ethnic group that is strong in tradition or special values?

Many of these answers can be found by listening and observing from the time you first meet the camper and parents. Once you understand this background, the camper's behavior will become more understandable.

One key factor that you want to learn through observation, listening, and perhaps from the registration information is the possibility of major traumatic experiences in the child's past.

Such experiences may include continual fear from city gangs, a divorce between parents, the death of a parent, parental abuse, parental neglect, overdose of TV, school failure or other troubles, and significant sibling rivalry or abuse. These kinds of things often produce a marked insecurity in the life of a child.

The child will handle this insecurity by forming some type of behavior pattern that shields him from further hurt. Dr. James Dobson in his book, *Hide or Seek*, goes into great detail describing the many alternatives.

The basic thesis of the book is that a child will either learn to run away and hide (try not to be noticed, stay out of the way), or he will seek (be aggressive, act out, be pushy, angry).

When you meet a child that tends to go toward either extreme, be sensitive to the possibility that this child is hurting but trying to cover it up.

The principle for you to remember is that children who are insecure need CONSISTENCY in love and discipline. Every child needs loads of unearned love.

The behavior-problem child needs clear rules that are consistently maintained. This is easy to say, but you will need God's special grace to carry out this superhuman task.

Children of the New Millennium from A to Z

From the 1960's to the year 2000 there has emerged a new breed of children that disturbingly fit a common behavior pattern. This pattern is based on growing up in a society that lacks absolutes (i.e. no right and wrong as determined by God), an overload of TV and the negative values it teaches, parents that do not have time for children, divorce, a serious lack of sound Biblical teaching and inadequate self-discipline development.

Even though all children do not fit this new mold, most children seem to be strongly influenced by it. A few children still have the privilege of growing up in solid, traditional Christian homes, but even these children are influenced by their peers.

The following list should look familiar. It has a marked resemblance to what the Bible calls mammon (materialism) and the old nature.

Angry: Hot blooded, intense reaction, passionate in self-defense

Bored: Their existence is too hollow, but they don't know what to do. Self-centered living is boring!

Blind: Creation is missed. Usually quite unaware or unappreciative of the beauty of nature.

Confused: Often do not know right from wrong.

Complaining: Rarely satisfied. Want more. Want better. Think they were cheated or short changed.

Defensive: Cannot handle criticism well. Make excuses or lie quickly.

Demanding: Want their own way. Want the best. Want to be first.

Educationally robbed: Slower children cannot read. "New" math or English or social studies has been a disaster.

Followers, not leaders: Slaves to the group. Even if a "leader," very sensitive to what the group will want or do. Very concerned (worried) about what others think.

Friendless: Want desperately to have "true" friends, but do not know how to give.

Godless: Have lost the concept of God. God simply isn't. God is never needed in school. Therefore, no accountability, no fear of judgment, easily deceived.

Hurt and hurting: By parents who divorced, parental fighting, parent neglect, drugs in the home, alcohol in the home, fighting between family members (aunts, uncles, others), and direct abuse.

Identity crisis is back! Where do they fit in? What is their purpose?

Integrity: What's that? Not embarrassed about anything. Don't blush. Use any words, tell any stories, wear any clothes.

Insecure: Will not venture out on their own. Will not take risks. Very afraid of failure. "No Fear" -- because quite afraid. But may "dare" that which is foolish to prove themselves to their peers.

Irresponsible: Do not take responsibility, usually blame others.

Judgmental: Critical and fault-finding of others: Accusing, hurt others verbally, lash out

Knowledge is lacking: Very shallow and narrow knowledge base.

Lazy: Very few enjoy hard work. Most want the easy road.

Listen to counsel? NO! Lack of trust, pride, foolishness.

Love: An unknown concept. "Love" on TV is on a physical level. Do not think parents love them (rightly or wrongly). Do not hear, "I love you." Do not understand.

Materialistic: Well-developed through advertising, friends, school, parents and TV.

Non-attentive (short attention span): Used to fast moving TV commercials, TV programs and movies.

NOW centered.: Very limited concept of the future. Do not see implications of present actions to future life. Often they see no need for education -- see no use for what they are learning.

Opinionated: They are right and others must be wrong (including adults).

Purposeless: No direction. No goals.

Quitters: Easier to quit than to lose. Easier to quit than try.

Robbed of childhood. Forced to grow up too fast. Sex education in kindergarten! TV is rank with violence and sex.

Sad: Do not know real joy, go after the artificial (drugs, games, gang, video games, computer games, movies). The things that bring real joy are often lacking (true friends, real accomplishment, simple pleasures, enjoying nature, having fun just to have fun, ice skating, walking, etc.).

Self-centered: Introvert or extrovert. That healthy balance is often lacking. Their world is seen only in relationship to themselves. Others are second to self. When driving a car, they do not see the danger they may cause to others.

Takes: The tendency is to expect others to give to them ; they do not think in terms of giving to others. Very easily slip into the mold: "You owe it to me." (This characteristic varies with personality)

Undisciplined: The old nature rules. Each does what is right in his own eyes. Never was made to control the desires of the flesh.

Unfeeling towards others: Do not see how their response affects others. Easily hurt others by words or actions.

Unmotivated: "Why should I?" Always want a reward or payment. Guilt does not motivate.

Unvalued: Other people do not see the current or potential value.

Values: Not God, church, prayer, or the Bible! Friends, materialism, money, status, or sometimes a sibling is valued. Their own word has no value. Lying is "in." Whatever it takes to get what you want or get away with something is acceptable..

Wrong influences: Follow the wrong people, fads, commercials, music, and values.

X, Y, Z.: Not all letters fit this outline, and not all youth fit this description! These are patterns that are common in many, but few children would have them all. Most youth would have some. Too many elements of these are seen in even some of the best Christian kids. Do you see yourself in some of these? Check out I John 1:4-9.

How Birth-Order Sequence Affects Your Campers

FIRST BORN

Closely related to family background are the significant patterns associated with birth-order sequence. Studies in birth-order patterns major in the first (oldest) child in the family.

This child often tends toward being perfectionistic, reliable, conscientious, well-organized, critical, serious, legalistic, loyal, self-reliant, an achiever, and a people pleaser. Take the time to learn this list. You will see strong evidences of it in your campers.

The reason for these common characteristics is not so much genetic as it is in the parental handling of the first-born. He is given an exorbitant amount of attention, high expectations, and much praise right from the time he could smile.

For a first-born, any one of the above characteristics could become dominant because of the parental attention.

LAST BORN

The last born (youngest) may also evidence some strong and noticeable characteristics. If the parents and siblings treated this child as the baby of the family, he may become outgoing, affectionate, absent-minded, and uncomplicated.

This last born is often the clown that thrives on attention.

Their behavior can also experience a wide swing from being so loving and affectionate to being rebellious, critical, spoiled, impatient and impetuous. This behavior swing from one extreme to the other is often "normal" for this child.

These behavior patterns have been created because he was never taken seriously, or perhaps he was always seen as the smallest and weakest and youngest. So he compensates by attracting attention or by trying to prove himself to adults.

Note, however, that these children are often people-oriented and can be sensitive to others. With their focus on people and relationships, things in their lives get lost: "Where's my Bible? Did he take my toothbrush? Where's my other sock?"

THE MIDDLE CHILD

The key to every child after #1 is born is the sibling directly above him in line. Each child tends to be in competition with the one who is next oldest. He may try to copy or try to catch up with the older brother or sister. More often, he will try to be the opposite. If the older sibling is "Miss Spiritual," this child may show little or no interest in spiritual things. If the older one is athletic, this child may either be super competitive or stay clear of all athletics.

Usually, this second child is competitive in some way (trying to prove himself) and wants to avoid conflict (a peace maker). When you have a middle child, gently probe to find out something about his next oldest brother or sister. Listen for clues to see if your child is jealous, rebellious, competitive or in harmony with this older one. You will want to note how your camper compares himself in interest and abilities.

Not all children fit these general patterns of birth order. Many have a complex mix because of divorce, being the youngest child but oldest boy (or girl), being second or third but also the oldest in the "second family," and so forth.

In other words, birth-order significance is not always clear and a usable tool to help you understand a child. Use the birth-order significance only when you have a clear case, which is usually the oldest or youngest child.

For a complete treatment of birth-order significance, read *The Birth Order Book* by Dr. Kevin Leman.

Four Basic Personality Types

The fourth factor for understanding children is the personality type study. Like the birth-order study, a child who is STRONG in only one type will be easiest to spot. Most children are a mix and therefore more balanced.

The chart on the following page is a clear and abbreviated outline of the four basic personality types. It will help you know what to look for in children.

However, the younger the child, the more his behavior will be more in line with age-group characteristics. For ease in seeing these things in others, this chart is most applicable to older teens and adults.

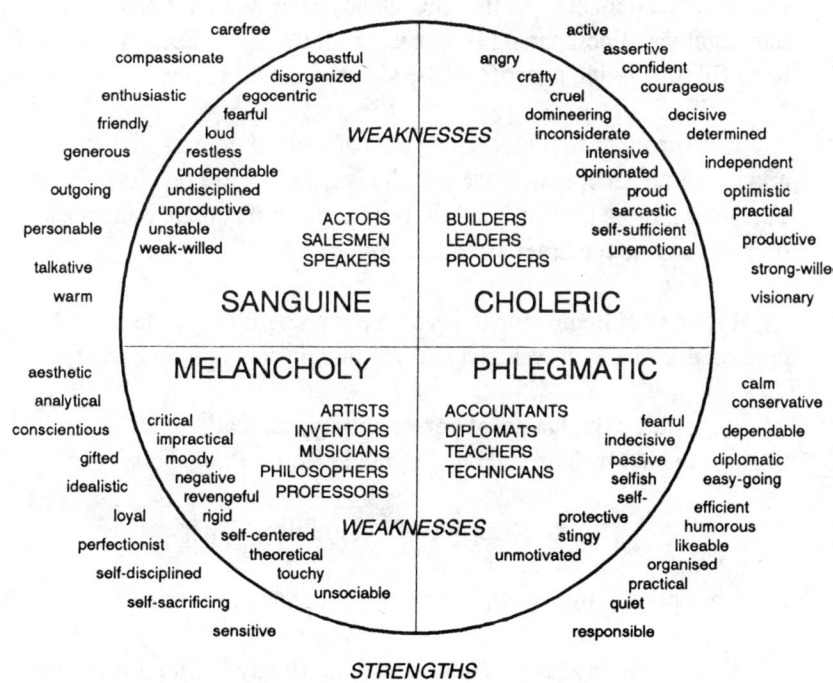

STRENGTHS

carefree
compassionate
enthusiastic
friendly
generous
outgoing
personable
talkative
warm

boastful
disorganized
egocentric
fearful
loud
restless
undependable
undisciplined
unproductive
unstable
weak-willed

WEAKNESSES

ACTORS
SALESMEN
SPEAKERS

SANGUINE

active
assertive
confident
courageous
decisive
determined
independent
optimistic
practical
productive
strong-willed
visionary

angry
crafty
cruel
domineering
inconsiderate
intensive
opinionated
proud
sarcastic
self-sufficient
unemotional

BUILDERS
LEADERS
PRODUCERS

CHOLERIC

aesthetic
analytical
conscientious
gifted
idealistic
loyal
perfectionist
self-disciplined
self-sacrificing
sensitive

MELANCHOLY

critical
impractical
moody
negative
revengeful
rigid
self-centered
theoretical
touchy
unsociable

ARTISTS
INVENTORS
MUSICIANS
PHILOSOPHERS
PROFESSORS

WEAKNESSES

PHLEGMATIC

ACCOUNTANTS
DIPLOMATS
TEACHERS
TECHNICIANS

fearful
indecisive
passive
selfish
self-
protective
stingy
unmotivated

calm
conservative
dependable
diplomatic
easy-going
efficient
humorous
likeable
organised
practical
quiet
responsible

STRENGTHS

If one of your campers (or fellow camp staff!) is clearly in one of the quarters on the chart, you have a wealth of understanding of that person.

If you are clearly on the opposite side of the chart, can you see why this person can be completely normal and yet so unlike yourself?

It is so natural to expect others to see things the way we do, but a basic understanding of personality types will help us see that God created each person to be unique. One type of person is NOT better than another. Each person is special in God's sight. Each was created to fulfill the Divine purpose of the Creator.

Use the chart to understand your campers and yourself better, and help you accept each one just the way he is. But do NOT force everyone into its neat little subdivisions. Even if someone fits 90%, do not assume the other 10% also applies.

I regret not being able to give proper recognition to the one who created this chart. It was given to me many years ago by a friend.

For a full explanation of personality types, read *Spirit Controlled Temperaments* by Tim LaHaye, Tyndale House Publishers.

An Example of Personality Types

Let's put all this together with one hypothetical example.

Bouncy Benny bounds into the cabin. Benny is friendly, not shy, a little fearful, and looks neat. The parents obviously are middle class and well-mannered. You can guess that he has had good upbringing and probably goes to church regularly. He may fit into the Sanguine type.

The parents introduce themselves, but when you check Benny's last name, you notice the parent's last name and Benny's last name are not the same. (You now realize that there has probably been either a divorce or death. There could be emotional scars and behavior patterns that try to cover up the hurts.)

In the getting-to-know-you conversation that comes the first day of camp, you find that Benny is the youngest of three boys. You conclude that Benny has the potential for being the spoiled baby of the family and or the "live wire" in the cabin. .

Before you label Benny as a spoiled, self-centered Sanguine who is insecure, you would do well to observe and listen carefully. He may NOT fit the picture.

If he does prove to fit the picture, at least you will have a much greater understanding of why he acts the way he does. As you work with Benny, remember the basic principle: children tend to live UP to our expectations or to live DOWN to our expectations. <u>NEVER label a child and then expect the worst!</u>

Conclusion

It is really exciting to see every child as a very special creation of God with a unique combination of these four critical factors.

As we begin to understand each camper, the approach we take and the expectations we put forth will vary with each one.

For those many children who are a blend of these many possibilities, we can expect them to NOT fit the mold that formed <u>us</u> as <u>we</u> were developing children. Each one will indeed be different and unique.

10   How to Handle Problem Children

This Kid Is Driving Me Crazy!

As a counselor, you may experience thoughts like these:

- "Omar is a clown. Everything is a joke with him, even the morning prayer time!"

- "Goula is a grump. Nothing suits her. I can't figure out why she keeps coming back to camp."

- "Billy is a bully. He's always on one of the smaller guys. He just can't leave them alone."

- "Teresa is terrible. She ALWAYS has to have her own way. The other girls are ready to drown her in the septic tank."

When I was a counselor, if a camp had 30 cabin units of children, one cabin would be ideal little girls who loved to sing, always learned their verses, behaved well at every meal, listened attentively in chapel, shared things, and helped each other. The other 29 cabin units were normal.

The normal cabin group would have eight to ten campers. Six will be moderately to well behaved. These six will usually do what you ask and earn a 90% on the ideal camper mental check sheet. The other two, three, or four will be in camp so that their parents can get a rest. These four campers make life worth ending.

Three Things You Should Never Do

This normal cabin with problem campers is usually handled in several wrong ways.

1. The counselor lets these few run the cabin by giving in to their demands so that he can keep the peace. This never works because this small group is self-centered and never satisfied.

2. The counselor uses all his time and emotional energy on problem children. This doesn't work because the other "good" children really don't have a counselor this week. They never get his attention, praise, encouragement or help because he is focusing on those that are a problem.

3. These few control the counselor by making him stern, aggravated, or even angry, but the whole cabin group must live with these attitudes. The counselor is thus reacting to the few instead of responding to the whole.

If you have an Omar Clown, Billy Bully, Goula Grump, or Terrible Teresa, take control of the situation before it takes control of you.

21 Things You Can Do When You Have a Problem Camper (or three!)

1. Find out what the problem is. Define it clearly. This is done by your careful listening and observing as well as by asking select and careful questions.

2. Discover the cause of the problem. Every problem has a cause that is not the problem itself. For example, two campers are fighting. The cause may include a basic selfishness, pride, a spoiled child, a neglectful home, basic thoughtlessness in picking on a weak child, or just immaturity and the old nature in control. If you, as the counselor, can't understand the cause, you can't do much to solve the problem.

3. Show the child the Biblical solution. It may take some explaining, but he needs to see God's way of handling life's problems. This assumes that you know the scriptures. This also assumes, that having accomplished the first two steps, you have the humility of a servant of Jesus Christ to admit you don't have a solution. Then the Camp Director or Camp Pastor or other resource person should be consulted. It is indeed tragic when a counselor has so much pride that he rarely goes for help to those whom God has provided.

4. Take care of the physical needs of each child. This is "preventive medicine."

Sleep: Follow the night routine. Insist on a full eight hours or more every night.

Diet: Do not allow the vegetables and fruits to be passed by at meals. Do not allow a heavy diet of candy and sweets. Sugar very often makes junior-age boys wild (hyperactive) and uncontrollable.

Exercise: Some campers avoid it. Encourage plenty of it. The first day, RUN every place you go with them and make it a game.

5. Take care of the emotional needs of each child.

Self-image: Learn their names, and use their names.

Acceptance: Do not allow one child to pick on another. Encourage total group activity.

Love: Pay special attention to each individual. By attitude and word, leave no doubt in his mind that you really do care.

6. Encourage self-reliance and accomplishment.

Don't do for him what he can do for himself. For little ones, express a "you can do it!" attitude and help him to do it right. Then follow through with praise. For older ones, treat them as adults and compliment them for jobs that are well done (cabin cleanup jobs, craft projects, learned verses).

7. For the child who is ALWAYS doing something wrong, pass over as much as possible, otherwise his camp experience will be like home and school _ overseen by dissatisfied and rejecting adult authority figures. In private counseling, help him to see his self-defeating cycle of behavior, and help him to choose alternative (Biblical) responses to problems.

8. Always be looking for an opportunity to praise and compliment. Even the seemingly proud and boastful child sees himself as worthless and unworthy.

9. Be extremely fair when giving out any form of discipline: a word of correction, a cross look, a penalty, anything. The problem child is always being blamed, but I have found that such a child is often "set up" by another more crafty child (or teen). The crafty one hangs back and privately smirks as the "victim" gets into trouble. Be careful. Never assume a child is guilty of an offense.

10. Give directions, rules, or expectations very clearly. Children, especially those who misbehave, often do not hear or do not understand what is really expected. Some disobedience may be a hearing or attention problem.

11. When children sharply disagree, they often try to settle it with a physical fight. "Might makes right" is their false value system. A frustrated counselor may want to sink to that level, too. Don't.

If you find yourself using physical force to make a child obey or to discipline him, you are wrong. Yes, there are rare exceptions, but you are safer following basic principles. Keep your battle on the level of will power, then you can always win while maintaining respect. You may win by using physical force, but you lose the respect of the cabin group, and a dangerous precedent is set.

12. Be WITH a child, never AGAINST him. Make a conscious effort to surround and approach every problem or problem child in such a way as to be clearly on his side.

For example, you might say to Billy Bully in a low and confidential tone: "Billy, you're a strong guy, and the other guys would like to have you as a friend, but you have to treat them right. By shoving them around and always trying to get your own way, you are causing the guys to turn against you. I don't want that to happen. What do you think you could do to earn their respect and friendship?" You are with him and on his side, but not approving his behavior.

13. De-emphasize winning and re-emphasize each success. A problem child is often the loser; so play down the camp contests. At the same time, notice good table manners (if you can find them!), a bed made well, cooperation given, effort put forth, or whatever positive thing you can find.

14. In private counseling, help him see the results of his actions. Gently, but firmly, make him take full responsibility for his actions and their results. Suggest or ask him for alternative ways to behave and react. A camper that's "driving you crazy" is a camper who is giving you multiple opportunities to counsel with him. In that private counseling situation, your first objective is to help the camper take responsibility for his own actions.

As you talk to these children, the common denominator is irresponsibility. They blame their actions and attitudes on their parents, the camp, the counselor, the other campers, or even society, but they themselves take no responsibility.

Your counseling should take this path: take responsibility, admit guilt, ask forgiveness of God, make it right with others. There is no growth in character without this path being taken. Christ died for OUR sins; it is personal.

15. Separate the child from the group. Because of high sugar intake, emotional disturbance, conviction of the Holy Spirit, a super giddy mood, home problems, lack of sleep, body chemical imbalance, or boredom, the camper may be giving you a very low level of cooperation and thus be destroying the spiritual emphasis of the hour.

Rather than reacting in anger, simply separate him. In chapel, put him in the aisle seat, and you sit next to him. In Bible class put him in the extra chair in the back of the room. In the dining hall, have him sit alone at the other end until the dishes are cleared. In the cabin after lights out, put him outside for 15 minutes if he is not cooperating and will not stop. (see the Night routine for details on this).

In any case, help him to understand why you are separating him; you cannot allow him to destroy this special time for others.

16. Help the child AVOID being disciplined by guiding him away from conflicts and problems. Keep him away from that other camper who always causes a conflict. Seat him on the end of the row. Put his bunk near yours. Assure his success any legal way you can. "Head him off at the pass" if he is going toward trouble. Work with him in this, and you will be his friend.

17. Always BE THERE! Most problems between campers arise because the counselor was not there. Lack of supervision is a major cause of accidents, too. BE where the campers are. This one principle will solve many, many problems.

18. Exemplify 1 Cor. 13. It's tough to fight against someone who loves you.

19. Ridicule, sarcasm, and negative jesting are sins that will destroy your relationship and destroy the child's self-image. Even though your frustration factor is running high, don't use these weapons. Don't ever use these weapons!

20. When problems do arise, discern the causes. Never take ONE side of a story. Work on the real problem.

21. Pray. It is the most important thing you will do all week.

What to Do with a Bully—6 Simple Steps

1. Don't be AGAINST this child. Protect the ones he/she is abusing. The bully needs to understand that you are not against him, but you will protect the others.

2. Never leave this child alone or out of sight. Alert other staff to help. Encourage the staff to have a positive attitude toward this one.

3. Take him aside privately and explain point 1 above, the camp rules and the consequences if he continues.

4. Give him a 24 hour test period restriction. (i.e., he cannot leave the counselor's sight without permission.)

5. Teach him that he has to give an account to God for all his actions (Ezekiel 18), and that God loves him and will forgive him if he repents.

6. If he repents, have the child pray for forgiveness and help in the future. If there is no repentance, you pray FOR the child and ask God to help him be the person God wants him to be.

This brings us naturally to the next problem, discipline of campers who misbehave. Before we jump into that often neglected topic, let's back up to "an ounce of prevention is worth a pound of cure."

Young people do not come to camp to be bawled out, yelled at, denied privileges, scolded, harassed, threatened, scared, and tortured. They didn't come to be the pawns of a power hungry counselor. They came to have a good time!

It's your job to ensure that this objective is achieved, as well as the camp's objectives of spiritual growth and character development.

You must keep the spirit of the cabin very positive with cooperation, excitement, anticipation, mutual respect, orderliness, and contentment to reach these objectives.

Take Nothing for Granted

The ideal cabin is created the very first day of the camping session. Some of your children have been coming here for years, but each counselor was different. Some campers have been to Camp WaHoo, where anything goes. Others have never been to camp.

On the first day, weld this group together. How? Give them a grand pep talk! Emphasize ours being the BEST cabin this week, the NEATEST, the hardest working, the sharpest, etc. Then explain exactly what is expected.

Never assume the campers know what is expected.

Go over the rules of the camp, the rules of the cabin, the expectations of obedience and cooperation, and who is in charge.

If you are laying down the rules, try to do it with some humor, and come around with them. Keep reminding them; they tend to forget easily. Show how all of this will help them have a good time.

Make the expectations quite clear: "When I am talking, you are not talking. When someone is talking to the whole camp family, all of us listen. When it's time to sing, everyone sings; even if you croak like a frog, croak loudly. Maybe there will be another frog in tune with you! Boys, stay out of the girls' cabin area at all times, no exceptions. When the bell rings, THIS cabin will be there first and look the sharpest. Right?"

When you give the pep talk and lay down the rules, try to make every rule clear for their own benefit. As their leader, you are 100% WITH them and for them. Keep your rules to a minimum, too.

Again, remember why they came to camp. There is no need to make a new rule every time there is a new problem; just work with the problem. A few basic principles can cover a lot of territory: be kind one to another; no physical contact; obey those in authority.

Here are the basic rules for the counselor who must make rules:

1. Make the expectations or rules known from the very beginning of camp.

2. Make them clear.

3. Make each one for the group's benefit.

4. Give them with humor and kindness.

5. Make as few as possible.

Five Ways To Get Respect from your Campers.

1. Follow the above 5 points.

2. Earn their respect.

Respect isn't earned by being physically big, by yelling, by having a title, or by lording it over others.

Respect is earned by reputation, by assumption, by conduct, and by maintaining the gap. Your reputation is what the campers think you are.

Word spreads quickly between campers: "Uncle Joe is a great guy, and he means what he says."   "Polly is a pushover. You can get away with most anything."   "Uncle Steve is never around. He's in love with Tilly, the life-guard."

Respect is earned by reputation. Be consistent from day to day.

3. Respect is earned by assumption. You must ASSUME your role as the authority figure and leader and thus tactfully demand respect that is appropriate for your position.

Many times you can observe a camper who quickly becomes the peer group leader. Watch closely and you will see that this child simply ASSUMES the authority to tell the others what to do, and they do it! Take command, and they will follow.

4. Respect is earned and maintained by your conduct. Are you deserving of their respect? Your conduct and general manners must be above reproach.

A camper will not respect a counselor who picks on the fat kid, assumes George is always guilty, leaves the cabin unattended, does a sloppy job in giving devotions, uses sarcasm and ridicule, or spends more time with his girl friend than his cabin of boys. Even a child will not respect the 250-pound Mr. Macho who behaves like this.

Respect assumes a looking up to another person. This means you must maintain the gap between them by being a leader and not a camper. There are already nine, nine-year olds in the cabin; they don't need or want a tenth who is chronologically over twenty. Being too much one of them is a sad but repeated mistake made by many counselors.

Here are some ways that you, as a counselor, can show respect and honor to each of your campers:

- Do not expect them to do something that you would not do for yourself or for them. For example, if cleaning the bathroom is part of the clean-up duty, take your turn or work with them.

- Never show favoritism toward any camper.

- Never gossip about your campers to others.

- Speak to them as you would an adult you admire.

5. Remember this, you'll never earn their respect if you don't also respect them! That's right. You must respect little seven-year old Dirty Face Danny.

Your respect is evidenced in the words you choose (no sarcasm), in your tone of voice (how would you address the guest speaker at a conference?), and in the way you give directions.

Do you order them around like a sergeant, or do you preface your request with "please" and follow through with a "thank you?" God calls each child by name. Do you? When they have a problem that is real to them, let it be real to you, too. Take them seriously.

Discipline problems can be prevented by an early and clear understanding of expectations, by earning respect, by giving respect, and by maintaining control.

How to Maintain Control

Someone will be in control, either you or a camper. Let it be the one God appointed. Control will greatly reduce the need to discipline, as well as maintain a good spirit.

Maintaining control is not as hard as you think. Put away the six-shooter and bull whip. They are not needed. Just BE where the action is.

If your campers are in the cabin, you are. If they are at the pool, so are you. Wherever they are, you are. Simple! Yes. Is this standard procedure for most counselors? No. If God has called you to this ministry, give it all you have.

Take your role as leader seriously, and your campers will take you seriously. Then when you speak, they will listen.

When a 200-pound sailor boy in full uniform walked into my cabin as a camper, I had to make a quick decision; "Who is in charge?" I treated him just like the rest, assumed my role as the leader, and had the whole cabin with me.

To maintain control, always be one step ahead of the group. When they plan that unofficial night visit to the girls' cabin, you are ready with a flashlight and a fake sleep routine. When their hand reaches for the door, suddenly the spot light goes on. "Surprise!" You are in control.

Here are a few more ways to prevent problems. I do not think you need any explanation, just a reminder: a basic attitude of humility, carefulness to show no favoritism, doing things with the camper, fairness in all decisions, a good sense of humor, a desire to serve the children (instead of being the big boss), not seeking applause or appreciation, a heart's desire to minister to needs, and a Godly attitude of love for every camper.

Remember, prevention is always easier than cure.

12

How to Discipline
With Love and Fairness

Discipline is not clobbering kids, making life miserable, or playing army sergeant. It does mean maintaining individual and group cooperation so that camp goals are accomplished.

If you follow through and use the preventive measures, will all discipline problems dissolve? Most books assume that you will not have problems. Ninety percent of the time this is true. Now about that ten percent .....

When Selfish Sally or Lazy Larry need to be brought back into line, the first step is to remind yourself and to explain to them exactly why you cannot allow misbehavior.

Four Reasons Why We Must Have Discipline

✓ **1**. Discipline is always for the camper. He is missing out on part of the fun and the heart beat of camp by not being "in" with the others.

His behavior is causing him to lose friends. If he is not corrected, he will be learning something that is wrong, and as God's representatives we can't allow that. He also needs training in self-control and subordination.

✓ **2**. Discipline is for the camp. One person can't be allowed to spoil things for everybody else. No one has the right to be destructive in any form (destroying property, spirit, attitudes, etc.).

Please note the attitude with which we approach the camper. We are FOR him and we are coming alongside him. You must make sure that he knows that we are not against him or he won't respond appropriately. Then the discipline will be ineffective.

✓ **3**. Discipline is maintained for the sake of the other campers. They have a right to security, safety, food, rest, a good time, and spiritual help. No one camper has the freedom to deny these things to others.

✓ **4**. Discipline is for the counselor. You need to maintain your leadership role and your position. However, never take revenge for something done to you, personally. Let another one in authority deal with such a problem.

We are back to the 10% who have the most wonderful counselor in the world (you!) and still cause a problem. What can you do?

First ask yourself why he is behaving that way. If possible, remove the temptation, situation, or surroundings that cause the misconduct. Then help him back on his feet and back onto the right track. Talk and pray with him.

Commonly Used Methods and Which Ones Work

1. *Do the easiest thing first.* Quite often all that is needed is for you to say something. Most problems could be avoided if the one in authority stopped the misconduct with just a word when he saw it developing. "John, that's enough. Stop, please," will usually end the problem.

2. Another method used is the ***"Big Stick" method.*** This method says: "I'm bigger than you, so you should do what I say." This does work, temporarily, but it often creates bigger problems of rebellion, disrespect, and antagonism.

Young, athletic, male counselors have often used this method. It seems to work because they see the boys responding. The positive response may be an initial admiration of Mr. Big Guy, but when the Big Guy isn't around, there is little respect.

Theologically, this method is against Scripture. Jesus said quite specifically that those in authority are not to "lord it over" those under them. So, even if you get good results, don't do what you know is wrong just because it works for a while.

3. A third method, used by frustrated and immature counselors, is *severe threats*. Put the use of threats in the context of all else that has been taught herein, and little room is left for them.

If you do make threats, keep these basic rules: (1) Always be prepared to carry them out, or else the camper will call your bluff. (2) Never threaten with a non-Christian punishment. "Either shut up or I'll stick your head in a toilet!" Would Jesus threaten that? (3) Never threaten beyond your power to enforce. The counselor does not have power to send a child home, spank, or deny meals. So when do you use threats?

Examples of Using a Threat

Rest time with free swimming or store time next:

"We have exactly 50 minutes left (with pencil in hand). When you girls are lying flat on your bed and quiet, your 50 minutes starts. If anyone keeps on messing around, she and I will stay and take our rest hour while the others go swimming." (You have thus made it a game, a challenge, and a threat. Be prepared to stay late!)

Meal time and one camper will not settle down or obey:

"Jody, you will either have to settle down and eat, or you will sit in the back corner of the dining hall until we have finished." (Be ready with a chair. Save the meal and let her eat when everyone has gone. Use this as a last resort.)

In chapel or at a campfire service, two children will not stop talking to each other or making a disturbance:

Either move over and sit between them or lean over to whisper to them. "You guys pay attention to Rev. Rightruth or you can have a special seat in the back with Uncle Firmhand" (Yes, DO move them during the meeting if they continue. No third and fourth and fifth warnings, please!)

On the playfield, Proud Pat is giving the others a hard time when they miss the ball. You call her to one side and tell her:

"Either you stop criticizing and cutting down the other players or you can sit with Aunt Lovenoball on the sidelines." Later or when she is sitting on the sidelines, use this as a counseling opportunity.

4. One of the most effective tools is the *"man-to-man talk."* (Woman-to-woman for you girls) You talk to the camper as one adult to another. This assumes your respect and assumes he/she is going to carry responsibility.

For how to use this time to its best advantage, refer to the previous chapter on counseling, but here are some general guidelines.

Discuss the reasons for the conduct and the natural consequences. The key to success is your approach and your mental attitude. You are working out a problem as an employer would do with an employee whom he trusted and respected.

Example: Sue Slop is the one who makes her cabin lose points because her bed isn't neat, and her things are not in order. You pick a time when it is just you and her, alone.

"Sue, the other girls really want to get honor cabin tomorrow. What do you think you can do to help?" No doubt the others have made it quite clear that Sue Slop is ruining their cabin record.

"Let's tackle this problem together. How can I help you have the neatest bed in the cabin?" Make it clear that you are WITH her, and not against her. You also need to teach her how to do some things, too. Make it a fun project that you do together.

5. Rather than calling them on every move, just *ignore their behavior*. This method requires a good supply of common sense. Children are children, and they act like it. Much of their so-called misbehavior is only childishness.

In every camp the counselors very soon find the one or more children who are ALWAYS doing something wrong. It seems they cannot even breathe right (it's into someone's face or "down your neck").

If you were to correct this child, that is ALL you would do all day, every day. For that child, establish basic and minimal boundaries and correct him every time these lines are crossed. You might call him aside after one day (the first evening) and explain.

"This is a Christian camp. We do things differently. We do not swear or tell dirty jokes. Fighting isn't a solution we use. We do not hit others. There's only one king of the castle (the counselor). It is imperative that you NOT scold him or verbally walk all over him. You are WITH him and want him "to have the best possible week, and this is the way to do it."

6. *"Diversion into fun."* This method is particularly good for the very young campers but will also work occasionally with older ones. Let's consider the older campers first.

One cause of disciplinary problems with older campers is too much free time. The solution is to have a camp program that is positively FULL of things to do. If you see trouble brewing, divert the group or individual into something fun to do.

- "I'll give my dessert at supper to the first one to the dining hall. Go!"

- "Let's challenge the Omaha cabin to a game of soccer."

- "Have you girls hiked to the maple grove yet? We have an hour, let's go."

- "Hey, the snack shop is opening in 10 minutes; let's beat the other cabin there."

- "Billy, would you play Frisbee with Hank?"

- "George, help me put this cabin back in order, would you?"

- "I'll challenge the winner at tetherball!"

- "Sam and Frank get the fire going. Bill, lay out the food. Matt, get more water. And the rest of us will scout up wood."

- "Would you find Uncle Heartful and invite him to eat with us tonight?"

If discipline in the form of punishment needs to be used, whether it's just a word spoken or cooling off time in the corner of the dining hall, there are basic principles of discipline that need to be followed.

Three Forms of Discipline <u>Never</u> to Use

Several forms of "discipline" are NEVER to be used. These forms come from the counselor's frustration, anger, immaturity, or plain old carnality.

1. Never use **ridicule, shaming or sarcasm**. These things are a direct attack upon the camper himself instead of correcting the action of the camper.

This gruesome threesome will help destroy the camper's self-image, may set negative examples for the camper to use towards others, will not change the behavior pattern, and certainly will be a negative influence on the counselor-camper relationship.

Sarcasm is so common between staff members that it's quite "normal" to apply it to campers. Sarcasm does not measure up to Scriptural standards of conversation. It is not kind, does not edify, and is not "seasoned with salt" as our conversation should be. If you would have others see Jesus in you, ALL sarcasm has to go. Sarcasm, even among staff, builds a negative atmosphere.

2. Never use **cruelty**. A few cruel counselors get so-called bright ideas how to make kids behave. They sit them under an outside light at night in their underwear and let them get eaten alive by bugs. They come up with other special events that should not even enter their minds.

Camps may have their own set of cruel and unusual punishments for campers. But is outright cruelty and fear a Godly way to care for children? On the contrary, Jesus even promised a millstone necklace with a deep-sea diving expedition for such practices.

3. Never **strike** a camper. These same immature counselors sometimes resort to hitting campers. It's the old "I'm bigger than you are, so shape up" philosophy.

As campers negatively react to a poor counselor or react against Holy Spirit conviction, the counselor is often the target of that reaction. How wrong it is for the Christ-representing counselor to respond in kind with vindictive punishment.

An easy-way-out kind of discipline is deprivation. The scenario usually goes something like this: "If you don't stop messing around, you can't go to swimming this afternoon! "

Deprivation means the counselor takes some normal camp activity away because the camper misbehaved. The child came to camp to have a good time, and now the counselor threatens to take away what the child came to get! This may be an entire meal, a dessert, store time, swim time, game time, or any other positive fun time.

Deprivation should be primarily the choice of the Camp Director or Supervisor over the counselor. It should, in any case, be used only sparingly and carefully.

The basic principles are these: any punishment should follow the offense quickly; and the offense and the punishment should be related. Deprivation may be appropriate if it is related to the problem (see point #2 below).

Back to Basics—Five Principles

1. Discipline should follow the offense as soon as possible. In a child's thinking, there is <u>no connection</u> (i.e., no response or change of behavior) between settling down to sleep on Tuesday night and losing swimming privileges on Wednesday afternoon.

Do something IMMEDIATELY if disciplinary action is needed. ***Do the easiest first: say something*** ("Frank, don't swing on the rafters; come on down.") If a child is talking during chapel, stretch your arm and tap him on the shoulder, or move over to sit next to him.

Do it NOW, rather than bawl him out later and take privileges away.

Suppose a child is misbehaving at the table after being spoken to several times. In the middle of his horseplay, take him away from the table to a lonely chair somewhere else. Don't wait until later to do something, because he will not remember what he has done or what his actions caused.

The child must get a mental and emotional connection between the misdeed and the consequences. A time lag can erase that connection.

2. Relate the misdeed to the punishment. If he disobeys the swimming rules, he sits on the ground by the lifeguard for 15 minutes.

If he doesn't eat the main part of the meal, he doesn't eat the dessert either.

If he wastes materials in the craft shop, he is charged for them or is limited in what he is allowed to do.

If he makes continued disturbances in Bible class, he is put in the back of the room next to a leader.

If he does not follow the safety rules at riflery, he is put on the sidelines for the period.

In all of these examples, there is no time lag and the punishment was appropriate for the misconduct.

3. Was the conduct WILLFUL or just CARELESS? If there is a doubt, trust the camper. Many things children (and teens) do is just childish carelessness. Such actions may be worthy of words of caution, but they do not merit actual punishment or deprivation of any kind.

At the table children spill things and make a mess; take time to teach table manners. At night in the cabin, they don't know what to do next in the night routine; guide them in getting organized.

In potentially dangerous camp activities (swimming, archery, riflery, canoeing) they do foolish things to copy something they saw on TV. Teach them basic safety and procedures BEFORE they can even touch the equipment.

Prevent and forgive carelessness; respond appropriately to willful disobedience.

4. Punish to the point of regret. The purpose for punishment is to make the conduct an unpleasant experience so the child will not want to repeat it.

You want to get the message across that it doesn't pay to misbehave. Whether you can accomplish this depends on the child.

If a tough nut has adopted the pattern of behavior that frequently breaks rules, the best you can do with any punishment is to make the misbehavior not totally rewarding and clearly not acceptable.

Above all, be fair. Do not overdo the punishment. Your purpose is to give EVERY child a great week at camp. You are NOT running a reformatory!

5. After a disciplinary action, try to pray with the child. He needs to know that you really do care and that your actions are for him and not against him.

Quite often during or at the end of a disciplinary action (set on the sidelines, taken out of the action, sent to the director) there is a great opportunity to counsel the camper lovingly.

Usually campers have experienced adult temper, frustration, or even abuse when misbehaving. Now, in this Christian camp, they get only fairness, love, concern, prayer and counsel. What a contrast! What an opportunity to exemplify the new life in Jesus!

Often, after a child is disciplined at home (i.e., yelled at and sent to his room), the punishment is seen as a result of the adult's anger, NOT as a result of his own behavior.

If you will follow these guidelines and basic principles, you can counsel the child into taking responsibility for his actions.

Taking responsibility is the FIRST step toward real change in behavior. I John 1:9 is not real to a person until he can accept his own responsibility for his own actions.

6. Administration of discipline is teamwork. The "Who" of discipline can be crucial to its effectiveness. You are the primary administrator.

In most of the examples given, you are the one who must administer discipline quickly, in relation to the offense, fairly, and with pure motives. But there are times when you must put aside your pride and humbly use other team members: a very serious problem, an ongoing series of problems, and camper abuse of the counselor.

What to Do When You are Abused by a Camper

When a camper abuses you, always arrange for someone else to handle the problem. If you correct the child, it looks to him like self-defense.

You must teach respect for authority; and you want to be always with him (on his side) and never against him.

If it is a minor incident (disrespectfully addressing the counselor, inappropriate jesting, ...), the Junior Counselor should step in and speak to the camper and reset appropriate standards.

If further action needs to be taken, or if the situation is more serious, the next higher one in the camp organizational structure should speak to the camper soon. This may be the Head Counselor, Program Director, Director, or Camp Pastor.

Your pride is the primary obstacle in the team approach to discipline. Pride says, "I can handle it. I do not need help."

Learn from My Mistake

I'll never forget sending a camper to the Camp Director. It was a teen snow camp in upper Wisconsin. This camper had a good supply of fire crackers. Repeatedly, he had been dropping them one at a time into the cabin's wood stove. I told him how dangerous it was, but he only waited for me to turn my back for a moment. This guy was incorrigible.

I lost my temper and marched him up to the Camp Director, a dear old grandfather-type saint and real man of God. I fully expected a royal bawling out for this camper and a few choice threats.

I was crushed. The director just sat this guy down and talked to him as a loving, kind, gentle, and understanding father. Of all the nerve! At the end of the week the campers filled out forms that included evaluation of the counselor. I lost the respect of the good kids when I lost my temper at the bad ones. I should have called for help sooner.

I learned four things from that experience:

1.   The higher authority does not and should not adopt the frustration of the lower authority. The higher the authority, the more God's qualities need to be evidenced.

2.   The lower authority needs to utilize the spiritual wisdom of the higher authority. One may be exasperated and not know how to deal effectively with a problem, but God supplies resources in his superiors.

3.   Teamwork in discipline needs to be used BEFORE the counselor messes things up.

4.   The camp leadership needs to back up counselors and not leave them stranded. The leadership needs to work closely with the counselors, know what is happening, and be a team that works together. In too many camps the counselor is on his own. This is a tragic mistake.

Teamwork

Teamwork can work for you and make camp doubly effective. When there is a problem camper (a camper who has a problem!), other staff can help, too. Yes, the kitchen girls, the craft assistant, and the maintenance guys, too. Enlist their help. Ask them to:

1. Be polite to him, even though the boy may be "asking for a nose job." Do not react, but respond. Give him what he needs, not what he deserves. Did not Jesus do that for us?

2. Learn his name and call him by name. Use his name! It shows real interest and respect. However tempting, do not use nicknames. Usually such names only increase the problem. I remember a fat little kid we dubbed "Butterfly Boy" because he seemed to be always chasing butterflies with his net. What he needed was genuine caring, not mocking.

3. Do not talk about him to others. Usually such conversation degenerates into non-complimentary "evaluations" that have a way of getting back to the camper. Once the child loses respect for the staff through this gossip, he will not be drawn to Jesus Christ. Is it worth the risk?

4. Pray for the camper. Give the prayer request to the staff in general and non-damaging terms. Avoid the traditional prayer meeting gossip session where they are only "sharing prayer requests."

5. Find time or excuses to talk to him: snack shop time, free swim period, before meals, when waiting in line, etc. The more that people talk to him as a person, the more we are working on some of the real problems such as low esteem.

Discipline is no fun for the camper or the counselor, but it is part of the counselor's job description. Without discipline, there is no learning. Chaos is the devil's tool. Orderliness is a godly quality.

If you must go further than just saying something, prayerfully hold onto the spirit of a humble servant who is serving His Lord.

13

How to Counsel With Campers

A counselor is one who works with others to solve their personal problems. You probably do not have a Master's degree in psychology. Neither do I. You have these children for only one week, perhaps two.

They come to you as total strangers. About Thursday, you feel you are getting to know them rather well, then they leave on Saturday! Sometimes their leaving makes you cry, and sometimes it's a relief! So what can you do to give them genuine help?

Rather than be a counselor in the professional sense of the term, you become an adult friend who understands and still loves. You can help a little toward that camper's understanding of himself and his relationship to God.

You can help that camper be more like Jesus Christ because your life touched his.

But to be truly an effective counselor.....

It's all in the heart!

The difference between a very successful servant and minister to children and youth and one that is mediocre or even a failure is how that person looks at each child under his care. Please allow me to speak from my heart to yours, and perhaps you can identify with my experience.

When I am face to face with a child (or teen, or adult!), what do I see? If this young person has caused me grief, aggravation, pain, irritation or a nervous break down, I may see a little monster that needs to be tamed.

What do I see when I look into the eyes of a child? Do I see a subspecies of the human race that is somehow not quite human? Or do I see a human being, an adult in the rough, for whom Christ died and whom Christ loves? Do I see a little villain that is bent on destroying my nervous system and ruining this week at camp? Or do I see a little person that is hurting on the inside because he or she got short changed on good parenting and a loving secure home?

Whether I fail or pass in the eyes of God as a successful children and youth worker, depends upon my heart. If my heart is not right toward this little person, then all of my skill, and all of my training, and all of my intellect, and all of my experience will be worth nothing in moving my camper toward Jesus Christ and Christian maturity.

As I speak to my camper, I need to see in this young person a 100% real person with emotions, and feelings, and memory, and past hurts, and fears, and a long future ahead. How I handle a problem, or how I go out of my way to give encouragement will NOT be forgotten. Children and teens are often super sensitive to facial expression, tone of voice, and use of words. These emanate from the heart.

Sometimes, we adults relate to children as if they had no feelings (i.e., yelling, using sarcasm, unfair punishment, anger, frustration at their stupidity or slowness or clumsiness). But how do we feel when our boss or our parents or our teachers treat us this way? We may say nothing. We may learn to not react. However, that hurt and that loss of respect do not go away. The memory of those cross words or that unkind act stays with us, too. News flash!! Children are people like you and me, and they react and feel like we do!

How do you work successfully with children? Remember the key that Jesus gave us: treat them just as we want to be treated. You want people to be patient with you. You want to be appreciated. You want others to notice when you do things right. You want to be forgiven when you mess it up. You want someone to show genuine care about you, to listen, and to come along side you. You want the security of not having to earn the other person's love. Those little people that call you "counselor" want these same things from you!

How do you see them? As aliens from outer space? As a major annoyance? Or do you see them as little people with needs and feelings and memories?

Sometimes I get caught up in the administration or the program or the fun of camp. Then for a time I look at my campers as a cabin group, or a team, or eight slippery fish to keep in line, or some creatures that are not really human. During those relapses, I get less respect, less response, less feeling, and less spiritual results from my campers. However, when I get my head and heart right, and I see every child as a vital and extremely important human being with great big emotional and spiritual needs, then I change how I relate to them. They change their response to me. I also start to pray more and fume less.

Counselor, to be a true success, it's all in the heart. Start with your heart attitude, THEN progress to counseling or discipline or leadership or whatever you are doing. Ask God for the heart of Jesus Christ as you look at each of your children. The methods and techniques in this manual just will not work well without it.

Let's see what the camper would appreciate in your "counseling" ministry to him.

What The Camper Wants from the Counselor

1.   *Campers want you!*   So build a relationship with each one. . With seven to ten campers in a cabin group, this is not easy. Try to learn their names before they come, and call them by name the first day. Make opportunities to help each one, to talk to each one, to listen to each one.

Avoid the temptation to socialize with your peer group (other staff, see "love" in the index). Instead, use the snack shop time or free time to get next to a camper.

Play with them in the pool or on the play field. Take time to teach them a skill: throwing a frisbee, coiling a rope, drawing a picture, or hitting a ball. In these and other ways, invest your life in theirs.

2.   *Campers want to be understood.*   You probably remember telling your own parents, "You just do not understand!" That lack of understanding built walls and not bridges. Your campers want you to understand them. You need to know their age group characteristics, but that's only the beginning. Get to know the individual camper by listening and observing each one carefully.

Remember, all behavior has significance. Every word the child speaks and every action he does will tell you something about him. Casually ask about family, school, pets, friends, and interests, but make careful mental notes on his answers.

3.   *Campers want your prayers*, even though they don't verbalize it. Set a goal and pray for each child at least three times a day. The better you know a child, the more intelligently you can pray for him.

4. *Campers want your attention*; they want your ear. At least once during the week, MAKE TIME TO TALK to each child personally and privately. After "breaking the ice" and establishing some measure of rapport, you want to ask: "Jessica, have you ever accepted Jesus Christ as your Savior?" "Can you tell me about it?" Your second topic could be related to the goal you have for her.

5. *Campers want your respect.* They are people. They do not see themselves as subhuman or aliens. They want to be treated with respect.

The One-on-One Counseling Time

Let's pause here and consider this private talk the counselor will have with each child, because it may be the most significant part of the week.

When to counsel a child is always a problem because the camp schedule is so full. Since the old devil knows it's an important time, he will be sure to leave you no time. There are at least ...

Nine Specific Times to "Make Friends" with Your Camper

Work on using these nine times effectively: free time, snack shop, swim time (by the side of the pool or on the beach), walking to or from the cabin, just before cabin devotions, after the evening meeting, during cabin cleanup time, when a question is asked, when a child stays back or lags behind, or when there is a fight between two campers.

A fight is a marvelous opportunity because the "good guy" image is dropped and character weakness is exposed. The specific problem between the campers gives you your prime example, and Scripture can be made to relate to this real-life problem.

When two campers get in a fight (verbal or otherwise), you have a golden opportunity to take each one aside ALONE and talk to him. The argument itself is only the springboard from which to dive into the real problems (if you can handle them effectively).

When campers do ask questions, are you ready to take advantage of that situation? Above all, be AVAILABLE. Always be ready to listen and to take time when it is important to the camper.

BE A GOOD LISTENER. Most adults just don't have time for children. Few adults ever really listen to children. Children (and teens) pick this up and read it as a noncaring attitude.

You can make this camper someone super special just by giving him your undivided attention. Someone once said that we should relate (that includes listening) to every other person as if he/she were the most important person in the world.

Listening well has a natural pitfall. Little Herkamera is beginning to open up and tell the counselor about herself and some of her problems. Counselor Go-Gettum Gretta gets emotionally involved in the problem, but can see some clear inconsistencies in Herk. Just the right Scripture verses flash into Go-Gettum's mind, and so she launches a Biblical rocket assault against Herkamera's problem.

When it's all over the counselor feels great (proud), and the camper learns to keep her mouth shut. Word spreads to the other campers, and they quickly learn to say as little as possible. The counselor then assumes that everything is just hunky-dory.

How much better it is for you to say nothing until you fully understand where the camper is coming from. Then use as many questions as possible to get your point across.

Five Basic Principles
When Listening to a Confidential Problem

1. Be ready to LISTEN. Ask leading questions and then listen with total undivided attention. You may be the fountain of all knowledge and have all answers for every child, but contain yourself.

2. Be on his level and do not use big words. Each age has its own vocabulary level and its own level of understanding concepts.

3. Have a positive attitude rather than an argumentative, or judgmental, or "know-it-all" attitude.

4. Stay neutral. All that you hear should be received with confidence and calmness. At all costs avoid the facial gasp and horrified look or shock. Beware, too, of the devilish delight in hearing the sordid details. In staying neutral, you will also not give approval for that which was sin.

5. Be honest and sincere. Admit you don't know, or suggest that this person see another who is more skilled to handle the special problem that surfaced.

You need to understand the person and the situation first, then direct them toward a Biblical solution or action. In other words, you are giving advice. Take it easy.

Since you are not in the place of God (all-knowing), you are running a high risk of giving incomplete or even wrong advice. So stay close to the Word of God.

You also need to help the person gain insight into himself to understand his own feelings, attitudes, and motives.

When counseling someone with a problem, be mentally looking for the answer: "Is there a change in behavior that the camper needs to accomplish?" Most problems can be helped by the counselee taking a different course of action or changing his attitude or response.

If this is the goal, you want that change not to be temporary (only for this one week at camp). This change may need to take place within the person himself: an attitude he holds, guilt that needs resolving, self-acceptance that needs nurturing, response to pressure that needs to be Christ-like, an old nature characteristic that needs to die, etc.

It may be that a change needs to be made in the context of his living: family, school, camp cabin, neighborhood. Do not overlook the possible need for change in the very nature of the person, from the old nature (without Christ) to the new nature.

Eleven Important Reminders

1. Counseling takes time. Plan for it. Make it happen.

2. Keep the confidence of the camper. Something may be humorous to you, but not to him. Take everything seriously, if that is the way it was given to you.

3. Maintain a cheerful objectivity. Getting emotionally involved will not help at all. You need to be thinking clearly and keeping the prayer channels open when listening.

4. To help him think things through more objectively, you may want to ask the camper, "Suppose your friend were in this situation, what would you tell him?" or "If I were in your shoes, what do you think I should do?" Everyone gives advice more easily than he solves his own problems.

5. Stay within your ability to counsel. Real problems can go into sincere self-image problems, guilt problems, home problems, marital trouble, and more.

6. Don't get in too deep, because far more damage can be done than help given. For the camper's sake, don't let pride take you for a ride at the camper's expense.

7. Expect patterns of behavior. For example, children often make little problems into big problems. The more you understand the age group with which you are working and chapter 16, the better counselor you will be.

8. Remember, not everyone thinks and reacts as you do or as you did when you were a child. In fact, there are five to seven distinctly different ways of handling life situations.

9. If you run into a counseling problem involving others, work out a solution with those involved after helping to straighten out the attitude of the one with whom you are working.

10. Encourage independence from you and dependence upon God. Some campers will want to become emotionally dependent upon you and always bring their problems to you. That is very flattering and really helps your ego, but it does not help the camper.

11. Make sure you follow up on any course of action that you suggest or outline.

24 Specific Questions You Can Ask That Will Help You to Understand Your Campers

To help a child, you need to understand that child. Here are some questions for which you will want to learn answers. You don't get the answers by nailing the kid in a corner and giving him the third degree.

You learn by watching with four eyes and keeping your ears open. Ask the following questions in casual conversation:

- What do you like to do? Any hobbies?

- Do you like school? What's your favorite subject?

- What church do you usually attend? How often do you go?

- How many friends do you have? Do you like being alone?

- Do your parents go to church?

- What does your father do? Is he home much? Does he play with you?

- How many brothers and sisters do you have? Where do you fit in?

- How do you get along with your brothers and/or sisters? Do you fight much?

- Do the other kids follow you or do you follow them? Do you get in much trouble?

- Have you ever accepted the Lord? When? How has the Lord affected your life?

- Do you pray? How often? Can you think of any time when the Lord has answered your prayers?

If you seriously desire to understand the camper, you will soon see that taking some kind of notes is imperative. In camp, it is often difficult to keep things confidential, so anything you write down must be carefully guarded. Never leave such a notebook or note cards lying around the cabin!

If you really want to counsel campers more effectively, put a real effort into studying the books by Jay Adams, Dr. James Dobson, or L.E.A.D. Ministries (P.O. Box 267, New Concord, Ohio 43762).

14 How to Lead a Child to Christ

Many times I have heard that camp is the place where many have been saved. In my own observation and casual polls of groups of Christian-school students, this seems to be changing. Now I find that many children from Christian families are accepting Jesus in the home.

Praise the Lord! That is the way it should be!

What this means is that the statistics for camps now will not look as good as they may have years ago. The danger lies in trying to manufacture situations where statistics can be raised (and later bragged over).

Let the Holy Spirit do His work where He will. If the home is the place of salvation, let us not be jealous, but rather be praising Him for parents who are doing the job.

So whom do we find in Christian camps? I believe we see two groups. First, we see non-Christians from non-Christian homes and schools.

The whole context of this group is secular: language, attitudes, music, dress and values. If one of these children becomes converted, he has large mountains to climb if he is to be like Jesus. The problems some face are almost inhuman.

The second group in camp are the Christian children from Christian homes and quite often Christian schools.

These children have the potential for great steps in growing in the Lord because they have a good foundation. Do not miss the opportunity to challenge these youth to commitment.

Can you see a potential problem with these two extremes in camp? The gap is growing wider all the time. At the same time, there is the real problem that our Christian kids are following the world.

Sometimes, a wise counselor with the right "mix" in the cabin can guide the stronger Christians to befriend and deliberately influence the new or weak ones. It's a new challenge!

When Are Your Best Opportunities
to Lead Children to Accept Jesus Christ?

It used to be that after the evening service the children would step forward to receive Christ. In some camps, this may still happen. Great! However, sometimes the weight falls on you to invite each child individually and privately to accept the Lord.

Many counselors now report that campers are being saved in the evening cabin devotions, during snack shop time, at the swimming pool, or with the counselor along a wooded path near the cabins.

The counselor can use MANY opportunities to talk to the camper about accepting Jesus Christ.

How?

When you have the opportunity to lead a child through the salvation decision, just what are you asking the child to do? We often use phrases like, "Ask Jesus into your heart," "Accept Jesus as your

Saviour," "Join the family of God by trusting in Jesus," and "Receive Jesus Christ."

John 3:15,16,18, 36; 6:35, 40, 47; 11:25, 26 and 12:46 all use the same word, "believeth."

That word does not mean a passive acceptance. It does not mean join the crowd. It does not mean a fire escape from hell. That word means to put one's complete trust and confidence in Jesus Christ.

It means to commit one's life to the person of Jesus Christ.

It means to accept the multiple invitations in John 3, 6, 11 and 12. To BELIEVE in Jesus Christ means that a person is putting his life into the hands of Jesus Christ. No wonder "old things are passed away."

II Peter 3:9 states that God is willing that all should come to repentance. Of course, God can then expect us to "be ye holy for I am holy."

The idea that a person can accept Jesus as Saviour without repentance and turning from sin and sometime in the future accept him as Lord is completely foreign to the Gospel of John. Inherent in "acceptance" is the concept of "repentance."

Perhaps we need to change our invitation: "Do you want to have Jesus take away your sin and be the boss of your life," or "Do you want Jesus to forgive your sin take over your life?"

What does Jesus do for us when we make this decision? Without getting too theologically detailed, let me suggest some basics.

1.   We are born again of the Holy Spirit. We have a new relationship with God and are called a son of God. John 3: 5-7 and John 1:12.

2.   We are sealed by the Holy Spirit. Eph. 1:13 and 430.

3.   We are baptized with the Holy Spirit into the body of Christ. I Cor. 12:12-13,25.

4.   The Holy Spirit now dwells in us. John 14:17 and I Cor. 6:19.

5.   We are no longer our own. We are bought with a price and should therefore be eager to glorify God in all we do. I Cor. 6:20.

God made the way of salvation so simple that even a child can find it. YOU can lead a child to Jesus Christ. When it comes right down to YOU and the CHILD sitting face to face with a Bible open on your lap, mild panic may set in, along with a blank mind!

Those beautiful seven-point and nine-point and even five-point steps to salvation suddenly are gone. Let's try a one-point and then a three-point method.

ONE POINT METHOD:

Receive Jesus Christ as your Lord and Saviour and "thou shalt be saved." That's it! That's all of it! So what are all the other points in the "plan of salvation" outlines?

They are simple scriptural steps to help a person want to be saved, or to explain more about salvation (i.e., need, repentance, not by works, assurance). For example, look at this three-point outline.

THREE-POINT METHOD:

•Show the child his need to be saved. You may start from ground level with Romans 3:23 and 6:23, or refer to a Bible study or chapel message that covered this area.

•Through John 3:16 and/or I Cor. 15:3,4 show him God's way of salvation in Jesus Christ.

•Lead him to accept Jesus Christ (Rev.3:20, John 1:12 & John 3)

Here are four other plans. Learn at least one.

FOUR-POINT PLAN:

•We are all sinners. Romans 3:23

•We must pay for our sins. Romans 6:23

•When we are offered a gift, we must reach out and take it. God is offering us a gift. John 3:16

•We must accept that gift. Rev. 3:20. John 1:12

Another FOUR-POINT PLAN could be:

•Come   Matthew 11:29

•Confess Romans 10:9

•Receive John 1:12

•Testify   Romans 10:9-10

THREE-POINT PLAN:

• Confess I John 1:9

• Believe Hebrews 11:6

• Accept Romans 10:9-10

ONE POINT PLAN:　John 3:16

God so loved the world. God gave his only begotten Son. Whosoever believeth. Should not perish but have everlasting life.

When it comes time to pray, there are only two alternatives, neither of which is foolproof. Tell the child to pray and suggest what to say.

Some children fully comprehend and pray beautifully and effectively. Most will just sit there.

If they do, try the second way. You pray and he repeats it. If somehow this does not seem meaningful, let's get back to basic truth.

If the Holy Spirit is convicting, the divine transaction may have already taken place. You are just sealing it for the child's memory.

Or, if he is really being saved by God at this moment, his heart and God's heart are speaking to each other and God isn't too picky about the words chosen by you or the child. YOU are not the child; God is saving the child. So relax, the whole thing is in God's hands!

There are sometimes one or two campers who accept the Lord on Monday night, and Tuesday night, and Wednesday night, and sometime during the day on Thursday if given the chance.

Why will a child keep coming forward for salvation? Usually, the approach taken is to assure the child of salvation by using appropriate verses like John 3:16, John 1:12   I John 5:11-12, and so forth.

It has been my observation that such a child is often one that is emotionally unstable or perhaps has the reputation for being the bad apple in the bushel.

In either case, I think the child is battling not with salvation and doubt, but with the problem of personal guilt. By repeatedly accepting the Lord as Saviour, he is having his sins taken away and the burden is lifted.

After the salvation assurance verses are used and explained, teach such a child to understand and use I John 1:9.

God never intended that we should carry guilt. He made a way to unload it. The child may also benefit from a study in Romans 6 on how to be "dead to sin but alive to God." The Basic Youth Conflicts material is excellent on this topic.

For information, write to Institute in Basic Life Principles, Box One, Oakbrook, IL. 60522-3001

The first goal for every counselor is that each camper would accept Jesus Christ as Saviour and Lord.

If you want that goal realized in every one of your campers, you will need to talk to each child individually within the first three or four days of camp and confront him with the plan of salvation or the opportunity to give his testimony.

Why You Never Fail

What of the camper that does NOT accept the Lord? What of the cabin of boys where four out of eight went home without accepting the Lord? Are you a failure?

Let's remember who does the saving in salvation. Can a clever person (you know, the salesman-evangelist) talk someone into salvation as you can talk someone into buying a new car? Sure! But that person probably is not saved.

Remember, salvation occurs when the heart of a person responds to the conviction of the Holy Spirit, and that person commits his life and soul to God through Jesus Christ. There is a turning around (repentance).

To "believe on the Lord Jesus Christ" is to make a life commitment and put one's life on the line. When that decision is made, the Holy Spirit comes in to dwell (takes up residence). That person is born again!

Now compare all that Divine activity in a person's life to the decision to "give into" the good salesman. His arguments are good. You like the product (heaven, no hell). "Sure, who would not want that. All I have to do is accept Jesus? Say a little prayer? O.K." The whole thing can be manufactured on the human level with no Divine intervention.

Back to our problem with the boy's cabin that went home unsaved. What happened? You did your job correctly; you prayed earnestly for each boy by name at least three times a day for the week.

Other staff members were alerted to the problem, and they were earnestly praying, too. These boys were enveloped in prayer, but did not know it.

The Holy Spirit, in response to this flood of prayer, brought conviction to each heart. God was tugging at them to come.

You talked to each one individually, but there was no interest or desire to come to the Lord. Since the boys were there only a week, we can only guess what prevented them.

Satan builds into even the youngest children bulwarks of defenses: disrespect for authority (ultimately God), poor father image (so God isn't understood), corrupted minds with rock music, TV. and comic books, peer pressure of the wrong kind, fear in many forms, belief in lies instead of truth, personal self-hate that actually turns a person against God, and the list goes on.

Some problems are so deep and so real, that one week at camp cannot rake through all the garbage in a person's life and get down to real soil where seeds of salvation can be sown.

What a tragedy if the counselor had pressured or tricked the boys into "accepting Jesus." Then all that God promised in salvation would NOT be theirs, but they would not understand why. What a mess would be created when God sent the next person along to lead them to the Saviour!

Your first objective is to win every child to Jesus. Whether or not that objective is reached is NOT up to you.

Your part is:

- to be a good, Godly example
- to pray earnestly and fervently for him
- to talk to him and give an invitation to come
- to encourage him to not close the door if he is not yet ready

Your cabin may be "all green" in the things of the Lord and know little or nothing at all. You then would have a very exciting mission field. Or, your cabin may be all church kids who know all the answers.

Whatever group God sends your way, just do your best as unto the Lord and leave the results with Him. YOU will not save anyone. It's not your job. Do not overlook the campers who have accepted the Lord and now need to make decisions that move them toward being more like Jesus Christ.

Expect great things from God.

15

It's been growing at alarming rates all across the country. According to a study done by the Los Angeles Times, as many as 13 million children (8 million girls and 5 million boys) will be abused before age 18.

You may have one or more of these children in your cabin.

Don't panic; you have plenty of support here at camp to help you deal with this problem.

Unless the child has come right out and told you of one or more specific incidents, please use the following list as a GUIDE ONLY. Remember, some of these symptoms may underlie other problems beside child abuse (i.e., lack of appetite may be caused by homesickness).

10 Common Symptoms of Sexual Abuse

1. Explicit (sometimes bizarre) sexual knowledge.
2. Precocious sexually related experimentation or speech.
3. Obsession with masturbation.
4. Withdrawal from normal human contact.
5. Suicidal depression; self-destructive tendencies.
6. Loss of appetite (this is normal in day one of camp).
7. Unexplained bruises or injuries in genital areas.

8. Lack of self-esteem or self-worth (<u>many</u> other causes of this)

9. Frequent nightmares

10. Infections of the mouth, gums or throat. (Be aware of venereal disease of the anus or throat. Incidents are no longer uncommon in children.)

NOTE: These are <u>symptoms</u> and may <u>not</u> indicate a problem. So proceed with extreme caution! It is vitally important to your camper's welfare that you stay alert without becoming paranoid!

It may be when they are changing for swimming that you notice your camper has a number of bruises or other marks. It could be late in the week and after your camper has gained confidence in you that he/she confidentially tells you about major trouble in the home. You might have one camper tell you about another camper in your cabin who has been molested by Dad or Uncle.

3 Things NOT to do

1. Please do not try to counsel the child concerning this problem! Don't take the risk of doing more harm than good! The hurts, emotions and feelings run very deep. Child abuse takes special care in counseling. Be a good listener and be sure to show compassion. Let the child confide in you. The child obviously has to get this burden "off his shoulders."

2. It's juicy gossip and makes a great story to tell the other counselors. Resist the temptation. Spreading such stories around only adds one more blow onto your camper. He has had enough already. Please, do not add to the hurt.

3. Do not play the part of Judge. It is not up to you to find out the details and truth of the story. Remember, some kids get into fights with other kids, so those marks and bruises might well be from such a fight rather than child abuse at home.

Child abuse is "popular" and creates much attention for a child; could it be that the stories the CHILD is spreading are false?

6 Things to do Right Away

1.   Take extra care to be sensitive to the child's feelings and thoughts. Some counselors like to horse around a little with their campers, but for an abused child this may be too close to real life horror at home. It may also stimulate unhealthy desires for a child who learned to enjoy the abuse.

2.   Take the problem seriously. It may be a misunderstanding on your part, but it is better not to take that chance. If there is the possibility of child abuse, act accordingly.

3.   If the child needs your firm arm around the shoulder (younger girls love to hold hands with counselor), give what is needed. Do not be afraid to give wholesome love and attention. At the same time, do not force it on the child.

4.   Lean heavy on the other campers to mind their own business if one of them sees the marks and begins to give the child a hard time. Come to the defense of the child and draw attention to some other subject. If the child wants to "brag" about abuse at home, stop it.

5.   Report your observations or suspicions to the Camp Director. Genuine child abuse, in most states, must be reported according to the law. This is NOT the job of the counselor but of the Camp Director. The Director may want to involve the Camp Nurse, but that is his decision and not yours.

What can you do for this child?

1. It is always appropriate to reassure the child of God's love and care.

Remember, the Devil is a real power in this world and does plenty of evil (see Job 1-3). Do not blame God for the Devil's work.

2. You and the Director may want to encourage the child to memorize verses on forgiveness, Jesus' blood taking away all our sin, God's love amidst trouble (see Psalms), and God's standards of conduct (Romans 12).

3. Sometimes abused children twist the blame and believe that they themselves are at fault. They think they are the major problem. Unlike what most other books tell you, the Bible says that we should confess our sins. Maybe there was something the child could have done. Maybe the child does carry some honest guilt. Guide the child through I John 1:9. Do what the Bible says.

Then reassure the child that he/she has taken care of the 10% that was his fault, and the adult must take the 90% responsibility. God has forgiven the child; the slate is clean. If we ignore or gloss over the 10% responsibility the child has, that child will continue to have a hard time not carrying the 90% that is not his/hers.

For more detailed information contact:

Child Protection Program
7441 Marvin D. Love Freeway, Suite 200
Dallas, TX 75237
(214) 709-0300

For Biblical counseling guidelines, contact:

L.E.A.D. Ministries (P.O. Box 267, New Concord, Ohio 43762).

16

How to
Love Each Camper

I Corinthians 13 Paraphrased

If I, as a counselor or staff person, speak like one of the great preachers when I feel inspired, or even if I should be as eloquent as an angel, but don't have that heart-deep love for the child to whom I am speaking, I'm just blaring like a trumpet in a junior high band, or banging like a kitchen cook on a pot to make symphonic music.

Or if I could foretell the future events in the lives of these campers and really understand the answers to the deep questions the children ask, and if I could have such great trust and belief in God that I could move mountains, just as Jesus said was possible, but really don't have a sincere love for those to whom I am supposedly ministering; I'm not a great person. Actually, I'm nothing, less than the smallest or most rebellious child.

If I give away everything I own to the poor children who come, and if I completely wear myself out, or should die in saving a young life; if I should do all this without love for my campers, it is of absolutely no profit to me; there is no reward in heaven. God does not praise me at all.

So what is love? How can I make my oratory and abilities and sacrifices really pay off and be worth something?

Love is putting up with the slow camper because he just can't do any better, or perhaps has never been motivated to try.

Love is looking for the little extra things to do or to say to those God has given me in my cabin.

When I love my campers, I'm not jealous when they prefer one another's company to mine. I'll just rejoice at the good friendships they are making.

Because I love these children, I'll not brag about my abilities or education or experience during cabin devotions. I'm more interested in them and what they think about.

Love is speaking to a camper on his level and avoiding the pedestal relationship. Even though they are children, love is treating them with good manners and courtesy. Love is sharing my life and sometimes my things.

Love is a calm word and an orderly response to four children clamoring for my attention at the same time.

Love is not keeping track of the wrongs that campers do, because I've forgiven them.

Love is being unhappy when one of my children wrongs another, and love is rejoicing when the truth is known.

One of the great things about love is that I can overlook the multitude of faults that each child has because I see the good that each child is trying to achieve.

Love means I can really trust that child, even though she may have let me down several times already.

Love gives me a vision of all that this precious child CAN be.

And lastly, love keeps me going 'till the end of camp so that every one of my children receives the very best of me.

Remember, I'm only a child.

(Seeing life from a child's point of view)

My hands are not skilled like yours. Please don't expect perfection when I'm making my handcraft, passing the milk, or playing with a ball.

My legs are much smaller than yours. Please slow down so that I can keep up with you.

My eyes have not seen nearly as much as you have. Many things are new to me, and many times I am going too fast and miss God's creation. Please help me see the beauty of the wild flower, the pureness of the morning mist, and the uniqueness of even the smallest of God's creatures.

My life is simple, and I don't understand all the things that you need to get done. Please take time to listen, to care, and to understand my simple world.

My feelings are quite soft. Please do not handle them harshly. They are closely related to my memory. Can you give me good memories?

Sometimes I'm kind of different from other kids in some way. Please treasure me as God's special creation that He put in your hands. Sometimes I need rules, sometimes guidelines, sometimes discipline, but I always need your compassion.

Being so young, I often do things wrong or don't know how to do them at all. I need your continual encouragement and patient instruction. Criticism really hurts because I try hard but fail often.

Yes, I make many mistakes, but that is one way that I learn. Please give me the freedom to make mistakes, but don't let me make very bad ones that will hurt others or me.

I like to do many things that you call work, so please don't take the pleasure out of these things by making them work. After I do something, please do not follow behind and redo it. That makes me feel as if I am not good enough and you do not like what I do. That is discouraging.

I'm so little compared to you, but I like it when you make me feel big. Thank you for talking to me in a way that says, "You are someone very important."

Someday, I'm going to be grown up like you. I'm watching you very closely to learn the right way. Please don't let me down.

17   How to Work with Children and Teens

Leading the Young?
How to get them to follow!

The following is a summary of many principles that have been covered and a few that have not yet been emphasized. To be an effective camp counselor or youth leader, all of these must be adopted into your leadership style and attitudes.

You will notice that many of these are not so much technique as they are maintaining the right attitude toward your ministry and your campers.

➤ Do It In the Power of God. Not only "do all to the glory of God," but do all in the power of God. When you do your part (yield to him, daily ask directions), God can do His part.

➤ Remind yourself of your supreme purpose for being here. This is vital for any ministry, and it ought to be done every day. This will make the necessary personal sacrifices easier to handle and will keep your energies focused on the things that are important to your Lord and Master.

➤ Give it all you have, but extend your strength to the last week by getting enough sleep, eating as healthy as possible (avoid the sugars), and taking a good dose of vitamins.

➤ Be prepared. Always be thinking ahead. Always be two steps ahead of the campers. Be ready before they arrive.

➤ Effectiveness with youth must come through relationships that have been built. The following four points explain how to build your relationship with each camper.

➤ Think positive about each camper. He/she is your reason for being here! Imagine what God would like to do in each life if only that camper would give God first place and total control. Let God rule in your own heart to love each one from the heart.

➤ Make every camper feel special. Learn every name. Do your best to be fair to each one, to talk to each one, to show a special interest in each one and ask questions that show interest and concern. Communicate by action, by facial expression, and by tone of voice that you do love each one.

➤ Pray for each camper. It will make the camper's attitude toward you much more positive (even if the camper does not know what you are doing!). Pray for your goal for each camper and for their needs as they arise during the week.

➤ Review chapter 16 -- How to Love a Child. The concepts in that chapter are critical toward developing a relationship and winning their respect.

➤ Make expectations clear. Lay down the rules as early as possible but in a positive and fun way. Never take anything for granted.

➤ Patience, understanding and wisdom toward campers can come through careful listening and observation. Develop both the habit and the skill of "learning" your campers.

➤ Real counseling is more than just giving advice. Do not be afraid to counselor campers Biblically, but know what you are doing. (Chapter 13)

➤ When handling problem campers, do not lose the others. Be fair, patient and loving to the offender. Give plenty of time to the good kids. Do not let the problem children destroy the group or the fun. The group as a whole is expecting you to protect them and maintain order.

➤ Praise for genuine accomplishments. It is important to "catch" a child doing something good. Emphasize achievement and character instead of competition and winning.

➤ Stay with the campers as a group. Find or make opportunities to be with campers individually. Multiple benefits include building relationship, showing concern, preventing problems, creating opportunities to counsel, and learning what each child is like. Ask yourself repeatedly: "Where are each of my campers?" Know the answer as long as you are on duty.

➤ Discipline when needed: do the easiest first, do not let a problem grow and develop, protect other campers, be fair, do not use belittling words, keep the conflict between you and the camper on the level of the will, and use teamwork when needed. See chapter 12.

➤ Being a godly example is basic to effective leadership. Keep your own life, thoughts, actions, and words pleasing to the Lord. They will not follow you unless they respect you.

➤ Let the campers do it. Before doing anything for them, ask yourself if there is some way that you could teach them how. They enjoy doing MUCH more than watching.

18 What to Do When Everything Goes Wrong

They assigned you a cabin, the one with the leaky roof.

Then in walked your Junior Counselor, Fanny Flighty. She couldn't figure out if she should put on a coat first or her shoes.

When you sat down in the dining hall, your chair collapsed. Your table was the last one to be served the spaghetti—cold.

When you asked for seconds (hoping it would be hot), they said, "We just ran out."

Then the Director asked you to lead a song at Vespers, the only song you did not know.

By the first night you knew your cabin of campers were all angels—complete with horns and tails.

The first week you were chosen by an anonymous kangaroo court to be the first one to take a pre-breakfast dip in the lake (the ice melted off just two weeks ago).

The second week was the same as the first, only perhaps a little worse.

Two of your campers must be rejects from the youth reformatory because they seem well educated in evil tricks and foul language.

Yours is the only cabin that scores perfectly for cabin cleanup; you never passed once all week.

The other counselors are praising God for the great response of their campers to the spiritual emphasis; your cabin can't seem to understand, "Why all this religious stuff?"

In riflery, the B.B. guns never worked, until your boy aimed at that girl walking by.

It did not rain all week, until it was your turn to conduct games after supper.

On the cookout they would not stop putting more wood on the fire. The Lord was good; the other cabin of boys put out the forest fire before it reached the pine grove.

The third week, fourth week, fifth week, and sixth week all were equally exciting. Nothing went right. You always got the worst cabin in camp. "Why me?" you asked the Lord repeatedly.

You begin to wonder if camp is some kind of penance punishment.

My second summer as a counselor was something like this fictitious experience, but not really that bad. For about five weeks I wondered why my cabin was always the worst one. Finally, I went to the Program Director who was the one assigning campers to cabins.

I asked why I always got the worst ones. He told me: "I know a lot of the kids because they have been here before. I give you the worst ones because you can handle them." That was great for my ego, but as I walked back to the cell, uh, cabin, I prayed: "Lord, isn't someone else able? I don't think I'm doing all that great with the boys."

It was years later before I realized what had happened. The Lord was preparing me for a life work with children.

By giving me child after child with problems, He was teaching me how to work with them and how to help them. If all had gone smoothly, many lessons would not have been learned.

Let me emphasize: "In all difficult situations, God IS sufficient."

When all is easy, we don't learn what God can do. "God is able."

If you find yourself always getting the worst, rejoice that God has a very special plan for your life that is the best! He is teaching you what most others will never learn.

You are someone special.

19 How to Work Within the Organizational Chart

It Gives Focus to Your Responsibilities

When you walk into camp, you have the right to expect that the Camp Director and supervisory staff have everything ready to go and are well organized. Whether this is the case or not, YOU have a job to do.

The point of this chapter is simply: Do your own job (ministry). Look back. That is a PERIOD after that sentence. DO YOUR OWN JOB, PERIOD.

The organizational chart may look something like this.

There is a Board of Directors at the top, then a Camp Director, then you as the counselor. In larger camps, it may be expanded with Assistant Directors, Program Directors, and so forth.

Someplace in all those little squares is one that says, "Counselors." That's you. Who is just above you? That's the person you go to with your problems or if you need help.

Trouble

A problem may come during the camp week when you see someone else NOT doing the job they are supposed to do, or at least not doing it the way you think it should be done. Is that person just below you on the organizational chart? NO!

You have only two alternatives: go to the one that is immediately over you and express your concern, then DROP IT; or ignore it and go about your own business.

This may sound a little heartless or even unchristian, but what happens when this advice is not followed?

Let's assume that no one in camp follows this principle. Everyone's business is everyone else's business.

During rest hour the counselor next to your cabin comes over and politely tells you to keep your campers quiet. You were having a serious discussion of how to know if something is right or wrong and one of the kids said something that caused the others to laugh.

You try briefly to explain this to your fellow counselor, but again his main concern is that rest hour be kept quiet. How do you feel right now toward that other counselor? How does he feel toward you? Is there peace and harmony and support and good feelings? I do not think the feelings are positive at all.

Your camp uses the waitress system in the dining hall. These girls serve the tables family style. You ask for another plate of pancakes, but she comes back with only two. You have a hungry table of campers! Only Two?!

Up to the kitchen you go with your plate and ask firmly for ten more pancakes. The dining room hostess tells you to sit down.

How do you feel toward that hostess and the waitress? How do they feel toward you? Is there peace and harmony and "esprit de corps"? Not quite!

How to Get the Most Out of Your Ministry

God has given each one in the camp a special ministry. If that ministry is to be done effectively, each one must give his all to his own ministry.

There is a basic principle in the business world: if you are to succeed, major in one thing at a time.

If you are to be a successful counselor, major in your ministry of caring for the ones God has put in your cabin group.

Let the other staff members take care of their ministry. If they let down on their end of things and it affects you, you can go to your supervisor with your concern, and then ask for God's grace to continue to do your best with the way things are.

For example, the rest hour problem could be solved in the Director's office or in a staff meeting by coming to an agreement as to just what rest hour policy should be. Whatever is decided, live with it joyfully. The pancake problem could be solved with patience. No one has died of hunger or starvation in a camp.

The Bible does tell us that we ARE to mind one another's business. However, the Bible admonition is in the positive. We are to care for those who are around us.

Words of encouragement to the other counselors, the waitresses, the Program Director and the Camp Director are always in order.

Many times you will see little things you can do to help (without interfering or taking over) other members of the camp family.

This leads to the last basic principle of organization. That you are responsible for those below you on the organizational chart (i.e., the campers) is obvious, but did you know that you are ALSO responsible for those ABOVE YOU on that chart?

You are not responsible to correct or direct, but you are responsible to make them a success. If the Program Director is your boss, what can you do to make him a success? What can you do to help him do his job a little better? How can you make his job easier?

The answers to these questions would be something like this: "I can obey his instructions, do my very best, stay with my campers, never be critical of him, and keep him informed as to what is happening in the cabin."

If your mental attitude is one of support for the one God has put over you, you will be amazed and happy at what you can do to help that person.

Doing God's work God's way always brings better results.

20 Little Extras That Make You Super Effective

There are some important things to know about being an effective minister in the Christian camp that do not take up a whole chapter. This chapter will collect all the little odds and ends. It may be one of the most important chapters in this whole book!

How to Be a Good Example

As a person who is now representing what a Christian is, you may be the stepping stone or the stumbling stone for a young life. The Christian camp cannot afford a bad example in the counselor's position. If the camp director is perceptive, he will give such a person a one way ticket home rather than risk the wrong lessons in the cabin family.

Being the example is no longer a cheap motivation used by the person in authority over you but becomes an absolute necessity.

We tell campers that Jesus is the answer to life, but do they see you struggling with problems or being rebellious against authority? We tell them to be quiet in chapel and rest hour, but are we talking or passing facial messages to friends? We tell them to sing as unto the Lord, but can they even hear you when you are right next to them? (So you have a voice that sounds bad even in the shower, let everybody hear it, and the camper will give singing a try, too.)

So like it or not, you DO have the responsibility to be the example. In fact, you <u>are</u> an example -- good or bad. Campers will watch you very closely.

Fun in the Kitchen

It sure looks like it, but that is NOT the place for counselors. Sometimes you see all that food going back and your table was a little short. It is so tempting to find an excuse to spend a little time in there. But are you an exception? Can others go there, too? Probably it's against the camp rules.

Every person who goes into the kitchen carries with him just a little more dirt, a few more germs, and probably leaves behind a healthy dose of confusion. Let the cook be a good guy. Don't even ask to be an exception.

How to Set the Spirit

You have had a hard morning. Lunch is late. At last you see that slowest waitress in camp finally getting to your table. Your tongue almost licks the platter as it is set on the table. Then you see it. Burned grilled cheese again! You don't need to say a thing; your face is as clear as the TV. screen.

What will the campers do? Probably they will pick up on your signal and reflect, "Yuck! Who can eat that stuff!" You set the spirit. What could you do to create a beautiful Christian spirit at that disappointing moment?

The camp schedule has a few minutes of free time before lunch. That special someone happens to be in the play area at the same time. You also see Larry Lonesome standing by himself. He's your camper. What will you do? O.K., what SHOULD you do?

The spirit of the camp should be the outward evidence and feeling that is spread around the camp because the Holy Spirit is working on the inside of people like you.

A great camp spirit is created when each person gives of himself to others. A selfless and self-giving spirit makes a great camp spirit.

What to Do about Practical Jokes

For some reason, "practical" jokes seem to burst out all over in some camps. Someone starts it and creates a good laugh. Another one picks it up; then there is some retaliation — do him one better. So it grows and grows. Did you ever stop and put all that in the context of Scripture? The "joke" is usually at someone else's expense. Very often it involves some destruction of property.

One summer such a spirit got moving in camp. Then one morning the young man who was helping with maintenance saw his prize running shoes cut to shreds and hanging from the flag pole. Funny? Not at all. He was furious and very hurt. If this spirit of "practical" jokes gets started in your camp, kill it.

If the joke is on you, ask God for the grace to accept it and then let it die without any retaliation. Most of these jokes are only a low way for one person to take out bad feelings toward another person. They do not belong in Jesus' camp.

Some camps have a tradition of playing jokes on the counselors. This can be done, but carefully. Such all-camp fun needs to have these criteria:

• It is for the campers' benefit and part of the fun of camp.

• It shows the campers how to be good sports (the one getting it takes it with humor, sets a good example).

• It can be an element in building unity as we play together.

• Such jokes are ALWAYS mild, never painful and never destructive.

An example would be the camp skits where someone gets a little wet in the "punch line." Sometimes a counselor has to "walk the plank," (walk off the diving board with a blindfold on) or just do something silly in front of the camp. It's all for fun.

Seven Sacrifices You May
Need to Make for Your Campers

Why are you at camp, anyway? The answer is obvious: to minister to the campers. Even though this is not new, keep this thought coming back to your mind repeatedly. Have patience with the Director and thank him for reminding you of this repeatedly all summer.

• If camp is for the camper, your dating life comes SECOND to that of time spent with the children.

• If food runs short in the dining hall, you are the one to go without.

• If the campers are lined up, you are last in line.

• If there is a fun activity going on, your job is to see that your children have a blast.

• If there is a ball game, you hit the ball only if all the other children have had a turn.

• If there is a contest, you step aside and let the campers compete, even if it means your team may lose.

• When lunch is dismissed, you don't tarry to talk; you move out with your kids.

"Lord, how can I make this special for my campers?" Make this your daily prayer.

How to Solve the #1 Problem for Long-Term Counselors

No, it isn't hunger! It certainly is not loneliness. Naturally, in a CHRISTIAN camp, the problem is a spiritual one.

In fact, if Satan can trip you up in this one way, he can probably make things go wrong like a row of dominoes falling against each other. If he can keep you from this one activity, he can almost destroy your ministry.

The number one problem? Counselors do not take time to have a real meaningful time with their Lord. Once a wedge is driven in there, the very power of God to do God's work, God's way, is choked off more and more.

The only preventive measure you have is to give it TOP PRIORITY. O.K., so you missed it this morning. How about rest hour? That half hour you have free in the morning? Just before supper? You can make the time if the task takes priority.

Tackle the #2 Problem,
Counselor Exhaustion, and How to Prevent It

This problem can really undermine the effectiveness of the counselor. Even with the number one problem under control, this thing can wipe you out. The problem is exhaustion—Dr. Dave will give his prescription.

• Don't take two aspirins and call me in the morning.

• REST during rest hour. Let the other counselor take the campers or get a relief person to fill in for you.

• SLEEP AT NIGHT. Believe it or not, you will not feel like going to bed. Quite often you want to stay up later, talk, socialize, or read. However, what you need MOST is sound sleep.

• PRAY more fervently for the campers. The more you pray, the more you will love them and thus have patience.

• Pray for yourself. The Lord is your strength.

• Take a good dose of strong multiple vitamins every day. If you can take the Shaklee plan, you may find it even better.

• Have a counseling session with the Director of the camp, and perhaps the camp nurse to ask for a break of extra sleep time. Do not push yourself to the end, because then you are no good to anyone. Do not let pride take you on a dead-end road of self-destruction. Take care of yourself so you can take good care of the children God has entrusted to your care.

What to Do When It Rains

The barometer that tells whether the day will be sunny or cloudy is the expression on your face. SMILE and look for special opportunities when it rains.

Whatever your situation, follow these basic principles:

• Never say a discouraging word. It will "dry up" the fun.

• Praise the Lord, both inwardly and outwardly.

- Be prepared with an hour of activity in the cabin. It may take the camp staff a while to adjust.

- Listen carefully for special announcements over the camp's P.A. system or bell system.

- Remember, the camper is here for only five full days. We cannot afford to miss ONE day because of rain. Let's make the most of it.

- Review the little book, "*90 Games and Activities for Rainy Day*." The director or someone in the office should have a copy. Copy down some key ideas that you can use. Be ready!

What to Do if You Fall in Love at Camp

Is it wrong to fall in love in camp? One could hardly call such a great feeling and flutter of the emotions sinful. In fact, some counselors see a Christian camp as a "happy hunting ground" because only the best college students want to be a counselor all summer in a youth camp. The problem is, how do two people handle it when they "flip" over each other in camp?

The problem is so real and so very difficult, that in my multiple years of camp ministry, I have witnessed only a handful of couples who could really handle the whole problem well. How did they do it?

- They set their priority on their campers. When it was time to be with the campers, they were with their campers.

- They earnestly sought the Lord's help to control their feelings and the temptation to spend time together, instead of in their ministry to children.

• They planned. They found "loop holes" in the camp schedule when they could be together. For example, with some effort they arranged to have the same time off. Sometimes they were partners in teaching the same class to campers. If one really tries, he might even get his cabin of boys assigned a table close to her cabin of girls. Planning can really pay off.

• They maintained a "no-physical-contact" policy. When the relationship goes into holding hands, kissing, and embracing, the emotions and inner drives become jet engines too big to keep under real control.

• They agreed together how to do it. They set mutual policies.

More often than not the young couple are like two magnets. Somehow they always manage to be together. When this happens, the Director is quite suspicious that someplace a ministry is not being performed. When a Director sees a guy counselor and girl counselor at the drinking fountain and no campers around, he knows 16 children are being short-changed, and the potential for trouble in those cabins is very high.

Why are you at camp? To find a girl or boy friend? If the heterosexual relationship is your priority, it's time to pack your bags.

Campers did not come to camp to see the staff pair off. Parents did not pay hard-earned money to send their children to camp so the staff can find their "someone special."

The camp board did not spend hours of time and assume great responsibility so two immature teens could spend most of the day chatting about nonessentials and griping over the Director's harassment.

Camp is for the campers. Do not let that ol' Devil take you away from the ministry and blessing that God has for you while you are at camp. Finding a "special someone" can be God's added blessing for those who put Him first and do things His way, but the campers are always the first priority.

What to Do if a Camper Has a Crush on You

A word should be added about another love affair in camp — the camper who flips over a counselor or staff person. Such an occurrence can have a large measure of humor in it for the staff. But be careful of the child's very real feelings and needs.

As with any behavior, we must ask, "Why?" We can only guess that perhaps this child is starved for love, or perhaps she has been accelerated in sexual interests by TV, love stories and older sisters.

Whatever the reason, we want the best for that child, and the path he or she has taken for fulfilling their need is NOT the best. In short, don't encourage it. Be polite and kind and gentle, but do not approve of the crush.

What to Do if Your Supervisor Wants a Conference— with YOU

There are plenty of things that the one over you (let's just call him the Director) would like adjusted in some way. He may notice that you are scowling when getting the kids lined up for lunch. He may have been bothered that you did not sing (set the example) in chapel last night. (He doesn't know about the very sore throat you have been fighting.) Maybe he has heard about the rift between you and the counselor in the cabin next door and wants to get it straightened out.

Whatever the reason for the interview, take three steps to avoid getting a bad attitude over it.

1.   Stop and think before jumping to your own defense. Is there any truth in it? Do I need to change something I am doing? Perhaps you need only to explain the situation, like the sore throat.

2.   Praise the Lord for someone who cares enough to help you. Do what is asked. Now move on with the ministry God has given you to do. Don't dwell on it and make a federal case out of it.

3.   If you were misunderstood, try to talk it over with the Director. You may need to change the outward appearance. If you still feel you are right, rejoice that the Lord knows the truth. Now MOVE ON.

How Much Sleep Should You Get?

Some experts now say that teenagers need at least eight hours of sleep each night. But you say, "I don't FEEL that need."

True, most teens can go on five to seven hours a night for several days, BUT THEN, suddenly, they are out of energy. They are also "out of sorts" and impatient. Colds come more easily, as do problems. What happened? You can run on reserve energy for many days, but when it is gone, IT'S GONE! You can find yourself near fatigue, exhaustion, or even infectious mononucleosis.

In God's work what kind of shape should we be in? Our best! We want to offer God our best, not our leftovers.

Rather than make the decision based on feelings, aim for the full eight hours every night. Save that reserve energy for emergencies when you'll need it. They do come!

Even with eight hours a night, in a full camp routine, you will be using up your energy, but use it wisely. Be at your best right to the last day of camp.

21 How to Have Special Campfire Services

"They all leave after breakfast tomorrow morning, Saturday. Tonight is the big campfire. I am in charge of it. What should I do? Last year they had a very meaningful service. Should I try to do it just as they did it? Somehow, I just have not sensed that same spirit in the camp this year. In fact, it's quite different."

There is a very old and traditional last-night's campfire where each person takes a stick, stands by the fire, gives a testimony, and then throws the stick into the fire. I think the symbolism at one time meant that the person so doing was dedicating his life to Jesus Christ. As the stick was given up to the fire, they were giving themselves up to Christ.

The major problem is that such a service often corners a young person (usually done in teen camps) into saying something and doing something that is not from the heart. Unless the whole service is handled very carefully, the stick into the fire becomes quite meaningless.

Experienced and skilled leadership can still make this a very meaningful campfire service. If you plan on using this "stick-into-the fire" service, I would encourage you to seek mature counsel.

Let's save this special symbolic testimony time for those times when we have that very special camp week where the Spirit of the Lord is obviously changing many lives.

If you have one of those special camp weeks, it might be well to arrange just who will participate BEFORE the campfire begins.

For example, during Friday's rest hour, plan to have a testimony time in the cabin to share stories of giving one's life to the Lord this week. Then right after rest hour, ask those select kids who have a real testimony to share that at the campfire.

Explain to them the symbolism of the stick being thrown into the fire. Of course, leave room for decisions and testimony at the campfire itself. Let a young person give his testimony AFTER praying a prayer of dedication privately with an adult after the invitation.

Did I lose you? This is the order: service, invitation, private counseling and prayer, return to the campfire, public testimony and fagot. To be really meaningful, it all must be done carefully and prayerfully.

There are other alternatives for that last campfire, too. After singing the songs that were learned that week and other favorites, have a good message that sums up the week and ties it all together. Then ask for testimonies from just two of the staff.

This will break the ice and get it started. However, don't let the staff take over. They are a rather enthusiastic group!

Getting Testimonies

Getting testimonies in a camp where the Lord has been working is not difficult. A method that I have finally settled upon eliminates the "pop corn" problem and the no response problem. "Who would like to share a good word of what the Lord has done in his life this week?"

"Would you please just stand up right where you are?" (If this is the first time you use this, you may want to clue in two staff members just in case.) "There are two. Are there any more"? (No one has spoken yet.) "Three, four. Thank you, Bob." (By now there are about a dozen.) "We will start over here and work our way around. Please, speak up loudly and clearly. It's hard to hear out in the open. Jane, if you would start please."

As these folks give their testimony, you will notice others slipping to their feet, but group pressure is minimal. You may want to ask them to come up front. What happens then is that a line forms to one side and they speak one at a time or come closer to front and center.

If you notice that enough have stood and/or you want to avoid the group pressure, just say, "I think that we have to stop here. We have about as many standing as we have time for. Please don't give us a sermon. We want to hear what God has done for you this week."

So your services would go: singing, message, testimonies, prayer.

If you had a week with a group of kids who were basically not responding, or a staff that was not cooperating (a bad camp spirit), it is probably best to cut that last night campfire a little short and/or give the preacher more time to reach them with the Word of God.

No matter how you decide to handle it, you will find that spending time in serious prayer will make a difference. Let God work through you even while planning this last night together.

22

How to Have

Successful Cookout

Site Preparation

The cookout site itself needs to be prepared. Personally, I prefer just a place in the woods that is made by campers.

The campcraft books give excellent pictures and helps on how to make it safe, but take precautions to keep the fire from spreading.

If in doubt, you are safer in making a hole and building the fire in a hole. This method holds the fire in a small area when there is wind, holds the coals together for better cooking, and makes it easier to put pots or pans over the fire by using two green sticks across the top of the hole. When the cookout is over, it is easier to cover it all up safely so wind cannot fan the ashes.

The cookout site should also have a place to put the food, usually ten feet or more from the fire. Campers love to play around the fire, and rarely do they see their sneakers shoveling dirt into the food. This is the most overlooked "rule" at cookouts, but if you follow it, it makes the whole event must easier for you.

Don't yell at them; move the food! It is also handy to have a place, like a log, to sit down and eat. Keep the eating AWAY from the fire because plates that are set on the ground will surely end up with unplanned seasonings mixed in with the food.

A "Things to Include" Checklist

Before going on the cookout, you should have a check sheet. This is a written list of everything you will need on the cookout.

Do NOT rely on your memory or the experience of the cook (he has been doing it for five years). Check off everything in the box before you leave on the cookout. If the cook or the ones packing the box used a check sheet, just go through the check sheet itself.

Things to include: adequate proportion of each food for the number going, correct number of plates, knives, forks, spoons, cups, napkins, cooking tools like large fork, spatula, pot or pan, HOT PADS, knife, matches (one of the most often forgotten items), extras such as salt, pepper, catsup, relish, and 1 gallon of water for extinguishing the fire. What is needed will of course depend on the menu. Think ahead.

How to Set Up When You Arrive

When you arrive at the cookout site, you need to get set up and then delegate responsibilities. If it is not a prepared site, make the fire place, seating, cup hangers and so forth.

Your cabin may have taken an hour the day before to come and make it a special place (see the campcraft books for some great ideas to make this place special). Put the food a distance from the fire and make it clear that no one is to go into the food box except the counselor.

Now delegate the responsibilities: someone work with the counselor in setting up the food, others gather piles of firewood, two others get the fire going.

Sometimes, EVERYONE gathers firewood together. You want a large supply not far from the fire. Do not let more than two at a time work on the fire; it will go out with each one blaming the others.

Fire-Safety Tips

When children (and teens!) get a fire going, they apply the old axiom: bigger is better. This is the wrong place for that thought.

Keep control of how much wood is put on the fire. An old Peanuts cartoon has the little guy saying, "Ready for the hot dogs!" as he stands next to a fire eight feet tall!

A cooking fire is SMALL. The initial flames may reach a couple of feet, but the idea is to burn as much as you can as fast as you can to establish a pile of coals.

Wood should be the thickness of fingers, not as big as arms. If too much wood is put on, it will take too long to burn it all down.

If you are cooking with fry pan or pot, cooking can start as soon as the fire has a good start and burned down enough to put the pot on. Again, go back to the campcraft books for illustrations.

The point here is to watch the children so that the cookout fire does not become a bonfire or even a forest fire.

How to Get Your Campers Involved

Above all, when on a cookout, follow the basic principle that the campers do what needs to be done. They will NOT have a great experience if the old, "pro" counselor does it for them.

Let them make the fireplace area. Let them make the fire three or four times (it keeps going out). Let them set up the food cafeteria style with each one coming through the line to pick up his things. This system saves wasted food and assures equal portions. Let them cook the food. Make them clean up the mess. Let them put out the fire.

This is easier said than done. Sure, you will need to give them examples and show them how to do it, or do your own as an example. But let them do their own.

How to Keep the Spirit High

Keep a good spirit at the cookout. Rather than barking at a child for digging into the food box, just remind him that it is off limits.

You may go hungry because you gave your hamburger to the child who dropped his into the fire. (Usually the cook at home base will have mercy on you.)

The firebrands are always a problem, so just set the firm rule that sticks put into the fire, stay in the fire. You will have to keep one eye on that fire the whole time.

If all goes wrong, make light of it and build the experience up as an adventure.

Our group of boys had hiked to the hill several hundred yards from the home base. The meal that I had planned (the whole camp was in cabin groups cooking this meal) included corn on the cob roasted in tin foil and hamburger patties with potatoes and carrots and onion wrapped in tin foil and roasted. The corn was pre-wrapped. The hamburger was a "camper make your own" thing, so all the parts were sent. Then we discovered: "No tin foil for the hamburgers!"

It was a beautiful day, and this was going to be a beautiful cookout. Since I was the Camp Director and was supposed to be the expert, a solution had to be found. "Charlie, would you run back to the kitchen and get the tin foil?" He soon came back with the message that, "tin foil was in all the boxes."

It was tempting to "pull rank" and demand it, but such would not be right. "O.K., Lord, now what do I do. How can I cook these hamburgers?" The corn! It was wrapped in foil! Carefully each boy unwrapped an ear of corn. The cookout went ahead with each boy getting his own meal ready. As soon as the hamburgers were done, we put the corn on the coals. For you who have not done this, make sure the corn is in all its finest green coats and soak it well in water, then lay it on the coals and turn it over after ten minutes (unless it turns black before then!).

We took the corn out of the coals, unwrapped the green husks carefully, and feasted like kings. Sure, some were burned here and there, and some were not quite done, but so what!

The spirit of the whole thing was one of adventure and resourcefulness. No unkind words were spoken about the cook and no complaining about food. When a camper did say something, I responded with, "That's O.K.., a little burned spot doesn't hurt. Just eat around it. Can you taste that special flavor from roasting it in the husks?"

Before leaving the cookout site, make sure all the garbage is picked up and stuffed into the cookout box or bag. Carry it back to the garbage cans, but FIRST separate out the cooking tools and silverware. A gallon of water is always brought for a fire extinguisher. Leave the area clean and neat and smokeless.

Experienced counselors have another saying that is used at the end of less than perfect cookouts: "Snack shop time is coming!"

Whether it goes well or totally flops, have a good time with the children and LET THEM DO IT. Keep the spirit high.

23

How to

Play It Safe

Check List

The campers came to have a good time. The camp organization wants each to experience spiritual growth. Both of these objectives can be destroyed if there is an accident.

If a camper steps on a nail, breaks a bone, becomes seriously ill or experiences a large cut that requires hospital care, that camper is out of all camp activities for part or all of the camp period.

Careless Cal, the cool counselor, takes his kids on a dangerous climb up rugged cliffs. He has a monkey swing contest in the cabin rafters. He didn't control the firebrands (burning sticks) the campers waved around during the cookout. The milk drinking contest at lunch put two kids in the infirmary. By the end of the week it was hard for him to measure results because so many in his group missed whole days of camp.

The Camp Director requires safety to accomplish both camp and camper goals and to keep the high cost of insurance down. He does not need parental law suits that threaten the camp's existence.

Counselors, like Careless Cal, do not think about these things; they only want everyone to have a good time.

You are the greatest factor in keeping that balance between having fun and playing it safe.

You are the one who is right there with the camper most of the day. It is your responsibility to prevent accidents by keeping one step ahead of the campers and THINKING safety, ause the campers will not think safety.

As the days and weeks whiz past, slow down enough to check over the following list once or twice a week.

A safe camp will largely depend on a safety-thinking counselor.

In the Cabin or Living Quarters

Okay	Needs Help	
____	____	Are all exit doors clearly marked and working?
____	____	Is there a fire extinguisher handy and updated?
____	____	Are extension cords properly used?
____	____	Are there no sharp edges to run into?
____	____	Do you prevent running or horseplay?
____	____	Are the electrical circuits not overloaded?
____	____	Are there any heating devices near combustibles?

General

Okay	Needs Help	
____	____	Do you know what to do in case of an emergency? (i.e., fire, lightening, flood)
____	____	Do you know what to do if you lose a camper?
____	____	Do you know what to do if a camper gets hurt?
____	____	If you allow campers to have knives, hatchets, or hand saws, are they closely supervised?
____	____	Are camp games well supervised and refereed?
____	____	Do you prevent unnecessary roughness in games?
____	____	Are campers not allowed to do an unauthorized, somewhat risky activity?
____	____	Is there anything laying around on the ground that is potential trouble (nails, boards, glass, trash)?
____	____	Do you not allow running on slippery or rough ground?
____	____	For special activities like horseback riding, archery, and riflery, do you require that all the safety procedures be followed?
____	____	Are your campers carefully supervised in the craft shop if using knives or hot objects?

Hikes, Cookouts, and Campouts

Okay	Needs Help	

Okay   **Needs Help**

____   ____   Do you check to be sure each camper is properly equipped for the campout? Do you have a checklist?

____   ____   Is there a first-aid kit with burn medication?

____   ____   Do you have fire fighting equipment (water, rake)?

____   ____   Is the fire protected?

____   ____   Are all burning sticks kept IN the fire?

____   ____   On hikes, have you taught them how to protect their eyes from low twigs and brush?

____   ____   For out-of-camp or woodland hikes, do you require that no camper go ahead of the lead counselor or fall behind the rear counselor?

____   ____   Can you recognize poisonous plants?

Waterfront

Okay	Needs Help	
____	____	Do you allow swimming ONLY with a lifeguard?
____	____	Do you ALSO watch the campers?
____	____	Do you not allow overloading of boats?
____	____	Do you require every boater to wear a lifejacket?
____	____	Do you help keep campers INSIDE the boating area?
____	____	Do you allow boating only WITH proper supervision?

Health

Okay	Needs Help	
____	____	Are you alert to signs of colds and illnesses?
____	____	Can you keep their feet dry in cool weather?
____	____	Can campers be kept warm enough at night?
____	____	Do you watch for a balanced nutritional meal (what they actually eat)?
____	____	Do you control how much candy and pop are eaten at the snack shack?

____ ____ When changing into swim suits, do you casually check for signs of a rash (communicable disease) or signs of child abuse?

____ ____ Do you report this to the Nurse?

____ ____ Do you maintain your own personal hygiene with showers, deodorant and so forth?

____ ____ Do you get adequate rest, eat nutritional food, and avoid the sugars, starches, and oily foods?

How to Best Use

24 The Last Night of Camp

"A Time to Remember"

For the youngest junior age campers, the last night of camp "has finally come." These little people are anxious to see Mom and Dad the next day. They may also be very tired from being on-the-go all week. In some camps, it works well for this youngest age group to go to bed earlier than the others because they are so beat.

For the grade school age child, that last night comes upon him all too quickly. "You mean we have to go home ALREADY?" They feel as though they could just take up permanent residence in camp! On that last night their adrenaline may be flowing more and thus they are evidencing more activity; or they may be dragging from having had a wonderful, but exhausting week.

Cabin Devotions

If you have a super active group, calm them down by your tone of voice, your mannerisms, and your conversational topics. "Jim, what did you like BEST about this week?" Get one thinking instead of acting, and you'll begin to get the attention of the others.

You want to draw attention to what was learned in Bible classes, new spiritual songs that were learned, and any noticeable ways that God worked in their lives.

You are tying together the whole week, and want to leave them with the thoughts of God's doings this week. Jim's response may be related to the Olympics in the pool yesterday, but you want to direct his thinking toward the spiritual emphasis of camp.

For the junior-high and high-school age group, their thinking may be taking a whole different turn. Initially, they may have thoughts about never seeing that special friend "ever again."

Emotionally, for teenagers, a parting of ways is always forever. They have not yet experienced the wonderful ways in which God brings us back together again.

Some young minds may also be thinking of the one grand climactic practical joke that they can play (this depends a lot upon the type of camp). If this describes your cabin group, you may need to use some of the "Last Amen" methods in chapter 5 and alert your supervisor (head counselor or Program Director) so extra help will be available.

Your objective is to get their minds on what the Lord has done this week in camp. Have them share testimonies or tell what was most meaningful to them this week. End your devotions with praise to God for what He has done, and then challenge them by saying something like this:

- "Sometimes it is tempting to end a week of camp by cutting lose or playing practical jokes on others, but let's just think where such ideas come from. Do you think God inspires those thoughts?"

- "I can't help but feel that we are still in a spiritual battle, and the ol' devil would like nothing better than to destroy the work of God in your hearts by provoking some of you to riotous living and ungodly actions."

• "Let's not let the devil get the victory. Let's end this week on a high mountain with God. How many of you are with me in this?" Then have them raise their hands (make a commitment!).

Girl-Boy Relationships

Another problem in some camps is the boy-girl relationships. Perhaps your camp has maintained a no dating standard, or maybe the Director has allowed very close friendships to develop.

The guys or gals in your cabin may have their imaginations running away with them: "I've got to see him tonight. We can sneak out after the counselor is asleep."

If you sense this happening, talk to them something like this: "The best relationships are those in which God is honored. If we want His blessing, we need to do things His way. Tomorrow is the appropriate time to have the good-byes. God has a wonderful way of bringing two people back together if He has planned one for the other. Rather than think of this as the LAST time you will see him/her, think about when the next time might be." (Camp reunions, area youth meetings, retreats, next year at camp.)

It might be good to talk about "How do two friends part?" You can guide the discussion into covering such topics as praying together, writing and encouraging, maintaining standards (mutual respect), and trusting God.

The Last Night for the Staff

Some camps make the last night of camp for the staff a very special time. You will need to do all that you can to bring the summer's ministry to a fitting close. Gather several ideas (on paper to help clarify and abbreviate your ideas) of what God has done through your ministry or in your life this summer.

You still need to be the spiritual leader. Don't let the Deceiver trick you into letting down your guard on this last night. Make the ending of camp a spiritual high, not a grand blow-out.

A big, last-night party and a lowering of standards are often a normal (old nature) temptation. On the last night of camp, you need to have a special walk with God, and you should encourage the other staff members to follow your lead.

Get names and addresses and start the habit of praying for others. You now know many needs; so now you can become an effective intercessor.

Write to these friends and let the friendships grow. An old song says, "Make new friends but keep the old, one is silver and the other gold." I have found this to be true.

25

Even though the campers are gone, your ministry to each camper has not ended. Your life has had an impact on their lives. For the rest of their lives, they will remember their week at camp and YOU.

Take advantage of this most extraordinary opportunity. Extend your influence for the Lord. Here are a few options.

The Letter Written to Oneself

Toward the end of the week or during the last rest hour, have each camper write a letter to himself. Encourage them to include any decisions that were made during the camping session, the Bible class emphasis, the best from the cabin devotions, and best activities and songs from camp.

After they write the letter, give each one an envelope to address to himself. For the young children, you may have to address it or carefully check what they have done.

Have them put their letter in the envelope. They should seal it only if they really don't want you to read it because it is too personal.

Collect them all; check for correct and full addresses. Hold them for mailing later.

You can mail them in a couple of weeks or at the end of the summer to give each one a boost and encouragement. You could mail them at Christmas time with a Christmas card and personal note of encouragement from you.

The Form-Letter Followup

The Camp Director may have a form letter printed to be sent to each camper. If he does not, why not ask for his help to make this idea work for you.

The form letter reminds the camper of the key Bible challenges that week, the theme song, and perhaps a few special events or happenings.

The letter closes with a challenge to continue the daily devotional time and walk with the Lord. You send this letter to your campers and add one or two personal handwritten lines to each letter.

Birthday and Christmas Cards

Children love to get mail. After camp, send each of your campers a birthday card (on time!) and a Christmas card. You will need to be collecting the campers' names, addresses, and birthdays during the summer.

This distinctive act of love will be very meaningful to your campers.

Personal Notes

Nothing can replace a personal note from you. If you can do it, make a real effort to send a special note to each camper once or twice during the year. If you can keep up with it or if some children have special needs, make it much more often.

Emphasize the spiritual uplift of camp and encourage an ongoing walk with the Lord.

For some campers, they may be connected to the World Wide Web or INTERNET. Collect their EMail addresses and send little notes back and forth. They'll love it!

Camp Reunion

If your camp has a camp reunion during the winter, Christmas, or spring school break, make an extra effort to be there. Review your campers' names and go out of your way to talk to each one.

You had many campers, but they had only ONE counselor. Live up to their expectations of one who cares.

Bible Study

Many camps have some type of Bible study or correspondence course for their campers. Do your part to get your campers involved in this program.

You may need to get them signed up before they leave camp, or it may be your responsibility to give the director the list of your campers who want to be part of it.

For the sake of your children, follow through with these ideas or others that would work well for you.

Conclusion

You will need to keep track of the correct names and addresses of all of your campers, whatever method is used. The value of camp can be greatly extended if you assume the responsibility to FOLLOW UP each of your campers.

26

The Three Minute
Daily Review List

• Do your best. You are responsible to God only for what you can do. Minister as a missionary to every child in your cabin. Plead God's special grace to NOT complain or have a negative attitude. Be salt.

• Pray for your campers. Pray earnestly. Pray fervently. Get others to pray. Then counsel with them individually.

• Stay with your campers. Let the others horse around if they must, but don't leave your responsibility. Give your children all you can. Buy every minute. Never, never, never leave them alone.

• Press for help when you need it. If the director lets you down, work out an assistance plan with the Camp Pastor, Program Director or even the counselor next door. "When my kids are heard by your kids after lights out, come on over to my cabin and read the riot act. Then I'll do the same for you." ANY outside person carries a special weight of authority. Use it.

• Don't try to change the camp. Major on your kids and do your job. Let the camp go as it is.

God called you to be a counselor; and that takes all you have.

The Measure of Success

27 How to Measure Your Success

They are gone! Whether between camp sessions or after the last day of the last week, you are suddenly struck by the stark quietness. It is all over. Camp has ended. Were you a success? Did you do well?

Even if your camp has an effective evaluation program that will help you know, this list of questions will be a good self-test to help you measure your success.

Think back on the past week or the whole summer. Rate yourself: 1 = Very Low; 5 = Very High.

1. Did I give my best to my campers?   1 2 3 4 5

2. Did I give each camper adequate time?   1 2 3 4 5

3. Did I stay WITH my campers?   1 2 3 4 5

4. Did I pray for every camper every day?   1 2 3 4 5

5. Was I NOT bossy with my campers?   1 2 3 4 5

6. Did I counsel with every camper one-on-one?   1 2 3 4 5

7. Were my cabin devotions at night camper-centered?

    and without preaching?   1 2 3 4 5

8. Did I maintain my own time with the Lord?   1 2 3 4 5

9. Did I maintain a consistent Christian testimony

by living the fruits of the Spirit (Gal. 5)?   1 2 3 4 5

10. Did I get along well with the staff?   1 2 3 4 5

11. Did I fully support my supervisor and the

Camp Director?   1 2 3 4 5

12. Did I meet needs that were NOT my

direct responsibility?   1 2 3 4 5

13. Was I positive and encouraging?   1 2 3 4 5

14. Did I do something to improve my skill

as a counselor?   1 2 3 4 5

15. Have I added each camper to my prayer list?   1 2 3 4 5

16. Did I complete the camp's required evaluations,

forms and reports?   1 2 3 4 5

17. Did I leave my cabin or living area clean?   1 2 3 4 5

18.   1 2 3 4 5

19.   1 2 3 4 5

20.   1 2 3 4 5

For numbers 18 to 20, add the things that are expected of you in your camp this summer. Checking yourself each week will be very beneficial in increasing your camp ministry effectiveness.

28 More Resources for Cabin Devotions

1. For discussion, one resource is your own creativity in making up a story that will help the campers grow toward your objective. Usually this will be some form of character growth goal.

2. Aesop's fables have a long history of teaching youth. If you can bring a copy to camp with you, these very interesting stories never grow old and are great teachers. After the story, summarize it with a key Scripture and application.

> * The hare and the tortoise. (Slow and steady wins the race. Don't Quit!)
>
> *. The lion and the mouse. (Little friends may prove great friends.)
>
> * The crow and the pitcher. (Little by little will help you get what you need.)
>
> * The shepherd boy and the wolf. (People who tell lies are seldom believed when they do finally tell the truth.)
>
> * The ant and the dove. (One good turn deserves another.)
>
> * The dog and the bone. (The greedy often lose what they do have.)

3. Cassette tapes and stories are available from Focus on the Family. Their Toll Free number is 1-800-232-6459. Explain how you will use them and ask them for their recommendations.

These stories are often exciting and may not fit into the quiet time you want. Review them in advance.

If you use the tapes, you may find it works well to "cut" the story at a critical part and promise to finish it the next night or rest hour if everyone cooperates with you and goes right to sleep.

These resources do cost money, but you yourself will enjoy them greatly.

4. Naturally, your best resource is The Bible. What happened many years ago is still a great teacher to kids today.

The following passages are examples of stories that can be read. Be sure to read the story ahead so it goes smoothly when you read to your cabin.

•Genesis 37:12-35   Joseph and his brothers. Jealousy hurts many and helps no one. See James 3:16

•Genesis 45:1-8   Joseph's brothers come to him to buy food. (Doing wrong to others comes back upon us. We never forget when we have hurt someone else.)

• Genesis 45:1-8   Joseph makes himself known to his brothers. (It is better to forgive than get even. Everyone wins.)

• Ruth 1:1-18   Ruth's covenant with Naomi. (This is a beautiful example of true loyalty and friendship. Read the whole chapter for the context.)

•I Samuel 21:1-10; 22:13,18   David tells a lie and 85 people die as a result of it. The lies we tell often hurt many others.

•I Samuel 24:1-7   David plays a practical joke on Saul, but his conscience teaches him respect for authority.

•Esther   The whole book would make a great series for one or two weeks. Individual parts of the story can be used for one or two nights. Study this one ahead of time.

•Psalms   The whole book of Psalms is Hebrew poetry. Just reading one chapter is a great way to end the day. These chapters can be meaningful to youth: 1, 4, 5, 8, 18:19-33, 19, 23, 34, 37:1-9, 40, 91, 95, 100, 103:11-22, 112, 116, 119:1-8 & 57-64, 119: 97-104, 121, 127, 139, 145, 149, 150.

•Proverbs   This is a great book for the counselor to study and then share appropriate parts with the campers. This book was originally written just for youth!

•Daniel 1   Daniel makes a firm decision to follow his convictions. (1:8 is the theme— purposing to do right.)

•Daniel 3   The story of the fiery furnace. (This teaches to stand firm for what is right.)

•Jonah   The story of the man swallowed by a great fish. The book itself is a complete story. Study it in advance so you will be able to tell it or just read parts of it each night. Note the point of the book in the last two verses: have pity and forgive even the worst person if he turns from his wrong ways.

•Matthew 7:1-5   Jesus' teaching on why we should not be critical and fault-finding.

•Matthew 27   The story of Jesus' crucifixion. Real love and self-sacrifice. The ONLY way of salvation.

•I Corinthians 13:47   Love. The best definition of love ever given. (Charity = love)   This can be a great discussion starter for teens. Note how this kind of love is "commitment."

To communicate well with your cabin group, talk from your heart and not just your head. The closer you can speak from the experience of having put the Bible into practice, the more effective you will be, no matter what resources you use.

THE END

INDEX

A

acceptance, 86
attitude, 150
attitude,your, 8

B

be kind and thoughtful, 67
be prepared, 140
be ye kind, 65
behavior, 69
behavior,how to change, 30
behavior,understanding, 159
behavior patterns, 70, 119
Bible, use of, 17
Bible stories, 190
    cabin devotions, 190
Biblical solutions, 85
    I Corinthians 13, 135
bully, 89

C

cabin,in the, 12
Camp Director, 18
camp is for the camper, 154
camp spirit, 152, 153, 161, 168
camper
    calling home, 23
    discipline of, 16
    excuses, 36
    fears, 22
    fears of, 15
    feeling secure, 22
    friends,losing, 97
    goals for, 27
    motivating, 37
    needs of, 14, 85

    observing, 15
    potential, 140
    praying with, 22
    problem with, 62
    taking responsibility, 88
    the quiet one, 56
    tired, 62
    using proper name, 14, 110
camper needs, 14
camper reactions, 14
campers
    praying for others, 17
    new, 12
campfire,how to plan, 161
competition, 19
complain, 185
conduct of counselor, 93
control, 84, 95
cookout, 165
cooperate with God, 8
cooperation, 92
cooperation,not getting, 88
counseling, 22, 87, 140
counselor, 8, 11, 111
    a new beginning for, 10
    endurance of, 139
    example,being the, 151
    home problems, 61
    job of, 147
    love of campers, 135
    maintaining control, 95, 98
    peer group, 114
    principles to follow, 139
    reactions to campers, 14
    send for help, 62
    servant to campers, 111
    talking too much, 61

K

kitchen, 152

L

last night of camp, 177
learn their names, 11
listening, 27, 71, 84, 114, 116, 117, 140
love, 86, 89, 135, 157, 159, 179
love, how to, 13, 135, 136
love for each camper, 13, 15, 140

M

meal,first, 15
minist ry, 185
ministry, 181

N

name of camper, 11, 14
new campers, 12
night routine, 22

O

observations,your, 28, 84, 132
observe each camper, 15, 70, 114
one step ahead, 95
organization, 149
OUT it must go!, 8

P

parents, 24, 28
party, 33
pep talk, 18

plan of salvation, 125
positive attitude, 117
potential,your, 9
power of God., 139
practical jokes, 153
praise, 86, 87, 141
pray, 8, 13, 17, 27, 30, 31, 45, 61, 89, 90, 98, 107, 110, 113, 114, 126, 140, 156, 163, 180, 185
prayer, 38
prepared,be, 140
presence of God, 7
presence of God., 7
problem, 31
problem, homesickness, 21
problem,cause of, 85
problem campers,handling, 84, 141
problems, people, 9
problems,causes, 89
profile campers,how to, 70
purpose, 139
purposes of the camp, 8, 91

Q

question, 48
questions, 57, 59, 60, 116, 120

R

rain, 156
relationships, 140, 179
reputation, 93
respect, 66, 93, 110, 115
rest hour, 149
ridicule, 89, 103
rules, 19, 86, 92

S

Order Form

If you would like more copies of this book, please tear out this order form and enclose it with a check made out to the *MCELROY* PUBLISHING. To order direct, just call toll free **1-800-225-0682.** All orders are backed by an unconditional one-year return privilege. Please inquire, if interested, about the quantity discount schedule.

Qty	Book	Unit	Total
____	How to Be a Successful Camp Counselor	16.95	____
____	The Camp Counselor's Handbook of Over 90 Games and Activities Just for Rainy Days.	5.95	____
____	Mastering Leadership in the Christian Camp	14.95	____
____	Encyclopedia of Christian Camping	99.00	____
____	Children of the New Millennium	7.00	____

Tax of 5% applies to Massachusetts residents only.   Tax ____

U.P.S. 15% of order.   S&H ____

Total ____

Person Ordering: _____

Company/camp: _____

Address: _____

City/state/zip :_____

Phone: (___) ____ - _____

McElroy Publishing, P.O. Box 488, Shirley, Ma. 01464

1-800-225-0682